# RESULTS COACHING
## IN 60 SECONDS

**The Eight Step Accelerated Coaching System
for Business Coaches and Managers**

## Anne Thomas
### With Amarpal S Saran

# Praise for RC60TM

We increased our sales performance by 362% in just 8 weeks!

**Bruce Rioch, Barclays Bank Plc**
**and the UK's National Sales Manager of the Year 2004**

Can I just say that I found RC60 of great value, informative and practical, I like the simple but focussed approach to coaching that you advocate and it works!

**Phil Parker**
**Sun Microsystems**

I have worked with Anne Thomas on a number of projects and attended the Results Coaching Programme. The programme is dynamic and energising and provides an excellent framework for the development of essential coaching skills. Anne is a highly professional and competent trainer and coach, who delivers excellent results and ensures delegates gain maximum benefit from their time with her. I have no hesitation in recommending her to my clients.

**Debbie Bailey MCIPD**
**Human Resources Consultant**

This has clarified a lot of grey areas I have had in management and helped me understand people more. The Enneagram is great way of making it easier to get the best out of my team. I am sure the impact will be a better performance and a better karma in the workplace.

**Tanya Lopez**
**Senior Manager, The Sanctuary Covent Garden**

I was surprised and impressed at how much could be achieved in such a short time. The combination of some careful preparation, staying focused throughout, and asking clear questions, all helped to produce a really positive conclusion for both me and the coachee.

**Rob Allmark**

**Sun Microsystems**

Outstanding. Practical applications for individuals and teams that are transferable to the business.

**Senior Management Team**
**Champneys Health Resort, UK**

It makes a refreshing change to learn skills that I will actually be able to use!

**Senior Management GlaxoSmithKlein**

Thank you for a wonderful training - we all got a lot out of it and are using the techniques. In fact we even scheduled in a practice session in our last PDM meeting! It really does work, you'll be pleased to hear.

**Sylvia Fielding**
**Sun Microsystems**

Brilliant! I understand how to coach in 60 seconds and connect with a group of people.

Superb models that give greater clarity about the coach's role as well as great tips

Very relevant to my job, provided useful insight into practical use of coaching to achieve results.

I really enjoyed the simplicity and relevance to our business need.

**Area Managers**
**WH Smith Plc**

If you really want to be an effective performance coach – DO THIS PROGRAMME!
Fantastic life changing experience.

Very powerful yet simple concepts. An extremely useful experience, thank you.

Could potentially be life changing. Get more than you ever imagined out of it. The best course I have ever been on. Very worthwhile.

**Team Leaders Barclays Bank Plc**
**Greater London**

*Find out at the end of this book how you can experience Results Coaching first hand through our One-Day Open Seminars.*

# RC60TM Press Publishing 2004

**Ordering Information**

For individual copies please visit our website:
www.rc60s.com

For bulk orders and discounts please contact us directly at:

Results Coaching in 60 Seconds Ltd
960 Capability Green
Luton
Beds
LU1 3PE
Tel: 044 (0) 1582 635032

Published By RC60© Press Publishing in Association with BookSurge 2004
and Rend Graphics 2004, www.rendgraphics.com.

BookSurge, LLC
5341 Dorchester Rd.
Suite 16
North Charleston, SC 29418

Copyright© by Anne Thomas 1998

Results Coaching in 60 Seconds Ltd
960 Capability Green
Luton
Beds
LU1 3PE
Tel:   044 (0) 1582 635032
Fax:  044 (0) 1582 635312

First Edition 2004
ISBN - 1-59109-990-0

# About the Authors

**Anne Thomas**

During her fourteen-year career as a corporate sales manager, Anne Thomas developed a passion for helping people achieve personal and professional goals that they once thought impossible. With a strong determination to share with others her love of coaching, Anne found herself learning with the very best and most established corporate and sports coaches of today.

She now delivers her one-day foundation seminars, trainer accreditation programmes and keynote speeches to people and organisations worldwide, working with many blue chip companies and their management teams. She demonstrates how to effortlessly integrate fast and effective coaching skills into your natural leadership style with amazing results.

**Amarpal S Saran**

Amarpal Saran is Head Trainer for RC60© and has contributed much of his personal material towards this book.

One of the U.K.'s leading experts in the everyday use of the Enneagram, Amarpal shares his expertise as a consulting professional for major companies worldwide.

Amarpal specializes in one of the most important areas of development in business, that of emotional intelligence and stress management.

**For information on how you can book RC60© events through either in-company trainings or open seminars please contact:**

Results Coaching in 60 Seconds Ltd
960 Capability Green
Luton
Beds
LU1 3PE
UK
Tel: 044 (0) 1582 635032

Email: info@rc60s.com

*To Amarpal*

*Thank you for your unconditional love, patience, faith and support*
*My love to you now and always.*

*Anne x*

# Acknowledgements

To Mum and Dad - I love you both very much. Thank you for making life fun and caring all of the time!

To Jan – just the best sis in the world!

To Andrea – thank you for being my best friend and being able to enjoy the highs and the low of life's journey together!

To Piers – for being a truly wonderful mentor and a very, very special friend.

To Sanjay – for never letting me get away with anything and pushing emotional buttons that have helped to allow RC60 to happen

To Sofia Palleson – the finest coach I have ever had who supported and believed in me at the start of this new journey.

To Dane for being one of the most energetic mentors we have had.

Anthony Robbins, John Whitmore (GROW Coaching), Hale Dwoskin (The Sedona MethodTM), Robert Cialdini, Robert Allen and his team. True masters in their respective fields!

To our clients who have worked closely with us over the past 4 years to make RC60 what it now is!

# Foreword

I am delighted that Anne has decided to make her unique coaching model: *Results Coaching in 60 Seconds* more widely available.

As an experienced trainer and consultant Anne has worked with many different types of people in organisations around the world. She has used that ongoing experience to develop, expand and refine her unique coaching model to the point where now this model can be widely and effectively used by managers and supervisors everywhere.

*Results Coaching in 60 Seconds* encompasses everything a person needs to know about coaching. As a step-by-step guide this programme is ideal for business managers and supervisors although anyone can benefit from its insights and guidance-it can, in fact, be used as an excellent self-coaching tool!

Coaching is now recognised by management specialists as *the* most cost efficient and effective methodology for performance enhancement. To be successful though, the coaching has to be both effective and lasting-this is where *Results Coaching in 60 Seconds* scores the biggest hit. This simple, concise eight-step model helps to both massively accelerate *and* improve your coaching work by focussing on the subjects' natural preferences for learning and growing.

Using the ancient system of the Enneagram, Anne has shown that by understanding that there are many different ways of experiencing the world, coaching can be "tailored" to feel more "personal" and therefore be more effective.

This individual approach, combined with the discipline of the 8 step model in *Results Coaching in 60 Seconds* makes this coaching method the most practical and relevant coaching method I have seen anywhere for today's business people. Give it a try! I believe you will be impressed with the results you obtain and will notice an immediate improvement in your coaching effectiveness-irrespective of your experience. I recommend *Results Coaching in 60 Seconds* with great enthusiasm.

**Piers Fallowfield-Cooper**
**Chairman**
**Itsmobile**

# Contents

## Chapter Seven
## Stipulate - Creating a razor-sharp focus within yourself and others

- Are you and your Coachee aiming for the same Target?
- Goal Setting Models that guarantee Success
- Producing a Statement of an Achievable Outcome
- Using this Model to effectively Coach a Team
- Handling Emotional Resistance when goal setting
- How to increase Confidence when the Objective appears to overwhelm the Coachee
- Aligning the Objective to meet the Needs of the Business and the Individual
- Measuring the Immeasurable
- Summary for Stipulate

## Chapter Eight
## Evaluate - Identifying the 'Real' Performance Blocks and Gaps

- Where are you now in relation to where you want to be?
- Why this Step alone will always improve Performance.
- What is preventing your Coachee from moving forward?
- The Question behind the Question
- The Meta Model
  - Generalisations
  - Distortions
  - Deletions
- Knowing when to move on to the next Coaching Step
- Summary for Evaluate

# Preface

Using numerous tried and tested techniques, we have now developed a high impact business model that shows how to make Results Coaching in 60 Seconds© a highly effective tool.

People often have the skills and ability to coach, yet find themselves preoccupied with task-orientated activities. They believe they simply do not have the time to do the coaching needed and are convinced that it is quicker to just give direct instructions - little do they know that coaching can be successful in a matter of seconds.

After working for 10 years as Sales Manager, Anne Thomas, founder and director of Results Coaching in 60 Seconds©, realised that coaching principles for managers needed to be much quicker and easier to apply. She also identified a need for the coaching impact to be far more immediate.

Much of the training she received herself was delivered by specialist sports coaches and was certainly some of the very best coaching training of its time. But there is a fine distinction to be made between coaching people in a sports capacity - where they naturally have a strong ambition to achieve great things - and coaching people who come to work with often no wider purpose than that of earning an income.

Her role as Regional Sales Manager for one of the world's leading financial institutions required her to be able to inspire and focus people *instantly* to stand any chance of producing consistent improvements in both her own performance and that of her team.

After three years spent designing, delivering and testing her material, she now offers a proven model with invaluable insights, guaranteed to help managers and their teams to sustain high levels of motivation and fulfilment more easily and of course produce results.

2

Her aim is to provide practical, down-to-earth coaching training through a complete series of training programmes, books, audiotapes and resources for immediate practical use by people in business - in the 'real world' – and which produce results consistently.

*"Treat people as if they were what they ought to be and you help*

*them to become what they are capable of being...."*

Goethe

# Introduction

> *"A good objective of leadership is to help those who are doing poorly to do well and to help those who are doing well to do even better."*
>
> **--Jim Rohn**

It was 14 years ago that I attended my first training programme for coaching skills. At that time, the group were told that coaching would take an average of 20 minutes per session. During the first 4 years of my coaching career I think it would be fair to say my coaching sessions would take an average of 45 minutes and even then my success rate was probably no higher than around 55 percent.

"Why waste time coaching? Surely it's quicker to either tell them what to do or even just do the job myself? Why won't people just do what I tell them to do? Can they not follow simple instructions? I know my ideas will work and I am right so why bother coaching? It will take me years to master coaching to really be effective!" These are just some of the questions I would ask myself.

Having worked as Sales Manager for a major UK high street bank for 14 years, and now as Director of my own training company, I fully appreciate and understand the challenges of business management and leadership.

As leaders, our own level of success is limited to the level at which the people around us succeed. With more stress-related issues arising daily, managers now need to develop greater emotional intelligence, self-awareness and resilience to achieve the results everyone wants.

People who use Results Coaching in 60 Seconds effectively are like football referees or baseball umpires; they go unnoticed when they are doing their job right.

I trust these coaching concepts will allow you to understand and experience the magic and simplicity of coaching. Also, how to achieve high levels of personal satisfaction and enjoyment by integrating coaching as part of your natural leadership style, watching people around you willingly and successfully work together, being happy on a daily basis.

If you are a life coach then I trust this book will further enhance your skills and truly bring out even more of your natural coaching talents, making you even more successful.

This coaching system has been created to incorporate everything you need to know to be a fast and effective coach. Having completed over 40 coaching training programmes across the world, I do indeed know what is available to you in terms of coaching training right now. I also know exactly what is missing and this book aims to fill those gaps.

In my view, coaching needs to be simple, fast and practical for use through much of the day and not something that we use during review meetings and structured coaching sessions. Coaching that delivers results!

Integrate coaching into your natural leadership style and notice how it becomes so effortless and automatic you don't even have to think about it. Just like driving a car!

I would like to suggest that you do not believe everything you read. But, before dismissing any aspect of this book, take these tools for testing and decide for yourself which aspects work for you. Throughout this book you are provided suggestions that will allow you to determine for yourself the validity of these concepts. I call them Proof Exercises. Have fun with them.

Working with some of the world's finest coaches I realised that these coaches were all very different in their approach, and yet they also worked within some form of structure.

Results Coaching in 60 Seconds is not a prescriptive text which claims that coaching can only work if you do this or do that. It is about allowing you to discover a style that is natural and effortless for you and also using this flexibility to create a structure that helps your coachee achieve what he or she wants. It is not about following a rigid set of rules such that the coachee thinks you are reading off a list of questions. It is about being flexible in the choice of questions within a framework that effectively guides someone to their (and your) outcome.

By learning about our own and other people's natural motivation styles we can bring out the very best in our own coaching, and tap into the most powerful natural resources within people to produce amazing results. The best tool I have come across to assist us in understanding core motivations behind behaviour, and understanding how people are at their best, is the Enneagram and this forms much of the foundation of the model in this book.

You may have heard the phrase "treat others as you wish to be treated yourself". In my experience this is misleading. Coaching is about treating others as *they* wish to be treated. This means having a simple focused questioning structure and knowing their deepest desires. The results then take care of themselves.

Coaching is an art. People who have attended our Foundation Programme have mastered the fundamentals of Results Coaching in 60 Seconds within 2 days. During training programmes my team and I have proved that these principles work every time and the exercises in this book have been designed for you to discover the power of these principles on your own.

It is important that you fully understand and appreciate the differences between Coaching, Counselling, Mentoring and

Training. People often believe they are coaching when in fact they are not.

## Coaching

Timothy Gallwey defines coaching as unlocking a person's potential to maximize their performance. It is helping them to learn rather than teaching them.

Using questions, coaching draws upon hidden talents and inspires creativity. It engenders immediate commitment, responsibility and

accountability towards the objective.

## Counselling

A counsellor would act in an advisory capacity and give professional help and advice to someone to resolve personal, social or psychological problems.

Stories people tell of why they do not have the things they want focus them on the problems rather than the solutions. It is easy to listen to people's excuses and stories on a daily basis, but coaching is about *elegantly*, quickly and consistently guiding their focus towards the desired results.

When I first started coaching I often spent more than half an hour at a time coaching people to improve their sales and service performance. In fact looking back on it, at least 80 percent of the discussion was unfocused and pleasant chatter rather than a stimulating coaching session.

Be a coach not a counsellor! Business leaders who say to me that coaching takes too long often use a counselling approach to managing people.

## Mentoring

A mentor is an experienced and trusted advisor, who trains, counsels and shares his or her extensive experience in a particular field. Combine this experience with Results Coaching in 60 Seconds skills and you have one of the most powerful resources available.

## Training

*Definition:*  To give instruction, teach a particular skill through practice.

I have seen managers attempt to use their coaching skills to improve performance without providing adequate training beforehand. You wouldn't take a first time driver, put them in a car and begin asking them questions about how they think they can start to drive and manoeuvre the vehicle!

This is sometimes the reason why coaching is not working or is taking too long. You need to ensure your coachee has had sufficient training to perform to a minimum standard before you can effectively coach them to improve that performance. Know when to coach and when to train.

### *Train knowledge and coach skill.*

I remember many of us returning from our first coaching training courses and using the set questions and techniques we had been taught. Before long, quite a few of my fellow coaches had given up using what they had learned, because it did not achieve the reaction they wanted from their team.

Telling people what you have been learning and letting them know you would like some help and support in developing these skills is, I find, a very elegant way of avoiding negative responses.

## The five Rules Of Coaching

Before coaching anyone I always discuss the five agreements that help him or her produce results.

1.  Whilst my role as a coach is to support you in achieving the business and even some of your personal goals, ultimately it is your responsibility to commit and follow through with the actions.
2.  Wherever possible, know what you want, or at least have an idea of what you want before you approach me. It makes it easier and quicker for all of us.
3.  The more committed and honest you are with me the more I can help you.
4.  Let's have fun with coaching!
5.  If you are unhappy with anything or you are not getting what you want then tell me. I cannot change my coaching style if I am unaware of what is not working for you.

My commitment is to share with you as much as possible all that I have learned, which in turn will enable you to make informed decisions about your own personal style of management and coaching.

*We read only 20% of the books we purchase. Allow this book to be in the 20% of your collection that you read from start to finish and apply as many of the exercises as you can.*

I trust you will enjoy this book and I hope one day to meet you in person at our training events. In the meantime, I wish you all the very best with your coaching.

*Happy Coaching!*

Chapter One

## The Results Coaching in 60 Seconds Model and how it works

It takes less than one minute to travel from the bottom to the top of an escalator in most shopping centres or underground stations and it is something we do without thinking. Coaching can be just as fast and equally easy when you know how.

> *"Outstanding leaders go out of the way to boost the self-esteem of their personnel. If people believe in themselves, it's amazing what they can accomplish."*
>
> **--Sam Walton**

## The Model for Results Coaching in 60 Seconds

Handrails on any moving platform are there to guide you and stop you falling, and with this coaching model your handrail is your integrity. Without it you are walking a very dangerous coaching path and even the most minor of slip-ups can send you tumbling back to the very bottom. It may take you a while to recover depending on how much damage you have done to yourself!

Built on a solid personal foundation, you *and the person you are coaching* decide and agree EXACTLY where you want to go. Next, using a process of asking relevant questions, take either each step of the process in turn or select the one or two most useful steps that will move you towards the desired outcome.

There are three elements to a successful coaching interaction:

1. You will always make sure you are operating from your natural state (just being yourself at your best). We will go into depth about this later.
2. You will always have a specific and clear objective in mind throughout.
3. If appropriate, you may use all 8 steps moving from one to another or you may select one, two or more. With practice your intuition will guide you as to which step(s) would be the most effective to use.

In order to be effective with your business coaching, it is important to have *infinite flexibility* with your techniques. The person you are coaching will then never be able to anticipate what questions you will ask, when or what approach you are going to take. And not knowing or second-guessing what you are about to ask keeps the coachee alert and more open to your coaching.

With practice you will intuitively know which steps in the model are the most effective 'in the moment' to move a person from a place of 'I can't to 'I can'. What I love about this system is that there is no right or wrong step to use; so be open, flexible, and have fun.

## Summary of each coaching step objective

| | |
|---|---|
| **Relate** | Build and maintain strong rapport and open relationships with the people you are coaching. |
| **Stipulate** | Know exactly what the objective is and make sure that both you and your coachee are holding exactly the same picture in your minds. |
| **Evaluate** | Based on their core motivational style, raise the coachee's awareness as to where they are now in relation to where they want to be. |
| **Motivate** | Based on their core motivational style, inspire and motivate them to follow through with necessary action and maintain their focus. |
| **Formulate** | Brainstorm and create ideas about how they can achieve this objective and how they can access any further resources available to them. |
| **Demonstrate** | By rehearsing or visualising situations in advance, give the person an experience of what it would feel like to take the actions they need to take with confidence |
| **Re-evaluate** | Review their progress. |
| **Celebrate** | Understand how they like to be praised and congratulate great performance. |

Over 350 ideas are contained in this book, allowing you to build a flexible coaching skill set and that means you can use a different approach to your coaching every time and get great results.

## Asking the right Question at the right Time

It is the questions we ask ourselves which determine our thoughts. And in turn it is our thoughts which determine how we feel. So, as a coach what <u>must</u> be mastered is the skill of asking the right question at the right time. Only then can you direct the focus of the coachee to a positive outcome.

How many times have you *told* someone what to do and they have gone away and done what they wanted to do anyway? Telling is not coaching.

Questions serve to raise the coachee's awareness of the consequences (both good and bad) of their behaviour and encourage him/her to take personal responsibility for both their actions and the ensuing results.

Suggestions for the type of questions you can ask during each of the coaching steps are listed within each relevant chapter. These ideas will guide you on the focus of attention required in order to both complete and master that particular step. You will find it beneficial to create your own questions which may suit your

communication style better.

Remember, by always holding the objective in your mind's eye this will ensure your questions are useful, relevant and positive in taking the coachee in the right direction. Each of your questions must begin with one of the following key words,

Who
What
When
How

These are all 'open' questions, requiring a detailed response form your coachee and not just a 'yes' or 'no' answer.

In certain contexts I recommend you avoid using the 'why' question when coaching, as it may cause your coachee to become

defensive and emotional.

The alternative of replacing 'why' with 'what makes/made you' or "what reasons do you have" will soften your approach, avoid the problem of defensiveness and keep your coachee open to you.

In chapter 5, you will find a useful guide to questions to ask in response to specific statements and throughout each individual step you are also given suggested questions with which you can practice.

Effective questioning techniques are just a matter of practice and you can do this both during and out of coaching sessions. Dinner in the evening with family or friends can be an ideal time to find out what the people closest to you have been up to during the day and at the same time be a practice opportunity for your own questioning techniques.

Useful Case Studies in chapter 12 discuss practical ( real-life ) examples of how people apply Results Coaching in 60 seconds. Each Case Study is followed  by a breakdown of the steps being used at any moment in time.

Your aim is to have infinite flexibility within each step. To help you establish a clear picture of your current skills and knowledge within each step, we have designed a self-assessment questionnaire.

## Assessing your current Skills Levels

If you have completed any coaching training in the past then some of these skills may already be available to you. It is important, though, to know where you are right now and monitor your progress. Then you can identify which of the coaching steps are your strongest and your weakest points and therefore which ones to focus your development on throughout the rest of the book.

In a later chapter you will find a more extensive version of this short questionnaire, which will reveal more specific areas you can work on within each step.

For now, let us get a sense of how you would consider your skill levels to be rated in terms of each of the basic requirements and steps for Results Coaching in 60 seconds.

To do this:

1. Complete the questionnaire honestly and openly.
2. Add your scores together to give yourself an overall mark out of 10.
3. Review your results.
4. Identify the key strengths and areas for development.
5. Agree with yourself an objective and a timescale by which you can work to improve your score.
6. Keep these results safe and diarise a time to review your progress once more when you have completed the book.
7. Repeat the process regularly.

## Coaching Step                                    Self Rating 1-10

| | |
|---|---|
| **Natural State** – your ability to remain emotionally grounded, unattached and open when coaching. | |
| **Goal Focused** – your ability to create, specify and remain focused on a goal. | |
| **Questions** – your ability to ask appropriate and effective questions. | |
| **Relate** – Your ability to build and maintain strong relationships with people when coaching. | |
| **Stipulate** – Your ability to extract, clarify and agree a goal with the person you are coaching. | |
| **Evaluate** – The ability to assist someone in knowing where he or she is right now in terms of achieving this objective and uncovering exactly what is preventing him or her from achieving it. | |
| **Motivate** – your ability to identify and utilise a person's natural motivators to make it effortless for them to follow through with necessary actions. | |
| **Formulate** – your ability to assist someone in creating a realistic action plan. | |
| **Demonstrate** – your ability to give a person an experience of what following through with the action plan will feel like. | |
| **Re-evaluate** – your ability and commitment to follow up and review agreed actions consistently. | |

| | |
|---|---|
| **Celebrate** – your commitment to praise a person and build further momentum in their confidence and self-esteem. | |

## Getting the most from this Book

The most important element of this book lies in discovering your natural coaching style and we suggest that you spend more concentrated time reading chapters two and three. Once this has been done, you can then take the other chapters page-by-page and day-by-day to build an extensive range of coaching skills.

10 minutes each day is all it takes to read about each step within this model and commit to practicing that given coaching principle for the day. Cumulatively, you will very quickly develop an abundance of coaching resources within yourself.

The act of journaling your experiences at the end of the day is the most amazing self-coaching tool. By doing this you can accelerate your development, and increase your awareness of how changing your approach achieves even better results even more consistently.

## Summary for the Results Coaching in 60 Seconds Model

### The three most important things to remember:

1.      The three vital ingredients of Results Coaching in 60 Seconds are:

*Being in your natural state*
*Having a specific objective in mind throughout the coaching interaction*
*Selecting one or more of the appropriate steps of the model.*

2.      Review your own perception of your coaching skills regularly – at least once each month and work on the areas that will make the biggest difference to you and therefore your coachees.

3.   Increase your flexibility by learning and practising as many of the 300 tools in this book as you can.

# Chapter Two

## Your Natural State
### Being your best Self when Coaching.

"There are two types of ego, and wisdom or intelligence makes a distinction. Similarly we must be able to distinguish between genuine humility and a lack of confidence."
"One may mistake the two because both of these are sort of slightly humbling mental functions but one is positive and one is negative."

**The Dalai Lama**

Complete openness to the person you are coaching, to their ideas, abilities, personal beliefs and holdbacks, habits and opinions, **without judgement** is THE entire key to success of coaching.

The moment you judge someone, you lose more of your personal power and your ability to influence and coach effectively.

Too often in business, managers are too emotionally attached to the business results. So much is at stake: their performance rating, their bonus, their pride, and maybe even their job, if their team does not perform.

Have you ever 'wanted' someone to perform so well that the pressure of your expectation hindered their ability to produce results? Imagine having a strong preference for something to happen without any fear of the consequences of it not happening.

The ego and being over-confident can be dangerous. John Wooden was America's most successful basketball coach and he said,

*"I have never gone into a game thinking we were going to lose. Even though there have been games where the experts said there was no way I could win. Even if we were the underdogs I felt anything could happen. Often I was right."*

*"That's also why I never assumed we were going to win."*

Having a relaxed focus as this means when things are not working for you and others, you stay completely grounded. Thus you give yourself a perfectly clear perspective on the whole situation and gain access to your greatest natural asset, your intuition.

Being fully open with your coachee means giving him/her your complete, undivided and relaxed attention all of the time, so that you can pick up on the obvious and subtle signs indicating whether they are closer or further away from the desired result.

How often do you find your mind wondering about other things, when having a conversation with someone and ending up losing track of the conversation?. Maybe you were thinking about what you did last weekend or what you are doing next weekend or even remembering that the car tax is due by Friday, instead of giving someone your full attention!

Our thoughts are based on either past experiences or projections into the future. If you are thinking, then you are not listening to your coachee. It is not that thinking is not valuable it is just that when you are coaching someone your full and complete attention needs to be on what they are saying. You cannot think and listen effectively at the same time. The more 'in the moment' you are, the greater your awareness of the things happening around you.

## The Natural Coaching State

The emotional state you are in at any moment in time dramatically affects your ability to produce results. For the people you are coaching to trust and remain wholly open to you, managing your own emotional state consistently and effectively is vital.

By 'emotional state' we mean the way you are feeling; and this is made up of your

- Physiology - the way you are sitting, standing or breathing
- Language - the words you use, and the way you say them.
- Beliefs – generalisations about what things mean to you
- Focus – where your attention is. This can be guided by your beliefs, and at the same time you also have conscious control over where to direct your focus at any moment in time.

You know what it feels like to have a good day and you know what it feels like to have a bad day.

So, what does the natural coaching state feel like?
The objective of the next exercise is to give you an experience of what the natural coaching state feels like. You will then be able to recognise when you are coaching people from the natural coaching state and when you are not.

The subsequent information, tools and techniques will also give you 60 second tips on how to regain this emotional state when you become aware of the need to. The Enneagram provides you with all you need to know to increase your awareness of which personal behaviour patterns prevent you from consistently accessing this natural coaching state. Therefore, by using this awareness you will be quicker to spot warning signals and have the resources to access your natural state whenever you choose.

**PROOF EXERCISE**

I suggest that you work with a colleague who can read the instructions to you so that you can relax even more into the experience.

1. Either sitting or standing, place both of your feet firmly on the floor.
2. Take 3 deep breaths in and allow yourself to completely relax.
3. Focus on a spot on the opposite wall, slightly above your eye level.
4. Now, still focusing on the same spot, expand your awareness to the left and to the right of it.
5. Expand your awareness outwards and all around you and notice how thoughts drop away and you immediately become more attentive and receptive to far more information, even becoming aware of what is behind you.

In coaching, the "spot" becomes the person you are coaching. As such you are giving him/her your complete and undivided attention, whilst staying open to what is being said and what you are seeing - all without judgement.

This whole process opens up your mind to so much more of the relevant information that is coming towards you

I guarantee you will produce greater results with your coaching every time you do this. It requires no thought, just complete trust that the right things are happening, for the right reasons and at the right time. This is being 'in the moment' and asking the questions that will make a difference right now.

You will find the next three chapters dedicated to massively increasing your awareness of the limiting patterns and behaviours, which consistently prevent you from getting the results you want.

This level of awareness will increase your emotional intelligence and accelerate the application of the results coaching in 60 seconds model principles. By applying them you will produce results immediately.

## Emotional Intelligence and Coaching

Daniel Goleman defines emotional intelligence in terms of the following abilities:

- *Knowing your emotions*
- *Managing your emotions*
- *Motivating yourself*
- *Handling relationships*
- *Knowing others' emotions*

As a coach, one of your objectives will be to assist the coachee in accessing more resourceful emotional states from which they can produce the results they want. You can only do this if you exercise your own emotional intelligence. The person with the greater flexibility  has the greatest control over the outcome.

Every reaction has a consequence, good or bad, and produces an outcome.

Knowing how to manage our emotions, thoughts and behaviour to produce the results we want is a key to success in both coaching and life.

Consider this scenario:

## EVENT + REACTION = OUTCOME

David and his family are flying out to Africa for their long awaited holiday of a lifetime, but when they arrive at the airport they discover their flight has been delayed by 4 hours. (This is the EVENT). David is angry and upset because he feels this is taking time away from his family and begins to get cross with the ground staff, who can do nothing to help. (This is David's REACTION) His children, who are 9 and 12 years old, are upset and begin moaning to Sally, his wife.

In the next four hours an argument develops, and by the time they reach their destination they are not even speaking to each other because neither parent can stop the children from moaning and misbehaving. (This is the OUTCOME). It takes the couple 24 hours to calm down and really begin
 enjoying their holiday.

Now consider this,

## EVENT + AWARENESS + RESPONSE = DESIRED OUTCOME

Imagine a replay of the same event. There is still a four-hour flight delay to Africa (EVENT), but the difference is that now,. as soon as David becomes aware of angry feelings(AWARENESS), he first takes a deep breath. Then he recommends to his wife that they spend the time exploring the airport stores for books on Africa, having dinner and spending time with the children showing them what they will experience when they arrive. (RESPONSE).

The delay still happens, but instead of destroying the great feelings around going on holiday, a momentum of good feelings builds up and the children are even happier when they arrive. The holiday is a success from day one! (DESIRED OUTCOME).

> *"Look at that word blame. It's just a coincidence that the last two letters spell the word me. But that coincidence is worth thinking about.*
> *Other people or unfortunate circumstances may have caused you to feel pain, but only you control whether you allow that pain to go on.*
> *If you want those feelings to go away, you have to say - It's up to me."*
>
> **- Arthur Freeman**

While sometimes we can't control what happens to us, we can learn to control how we respond.

Like goldfish in a goldfish bowl cannot see the water they are swimming in, we are sometimes unaware of our limitations, because we are so involved in and attached to our own experience. Look at the bowl from the outside and then you can see the water clearly. I know some coaches who often jump into the bowl with the coachee! Your job is to stay outside of it.

Know how your behaviour is contributing to any situation, be it coaching or otherwise, and change your approach if your actions are neither improving nor supporting the situation you find yourself in. This is taking responsibility and using your emotional intelligence.

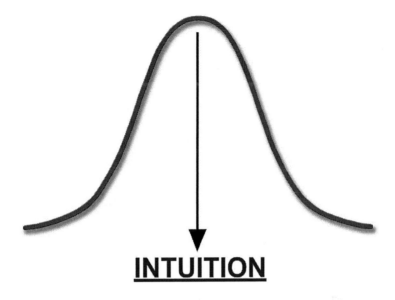

# INTUITION

The more relaxed we are, the closer we are to and the more naturally we make use of our intuition. The higher up this bell curve we are emotionally, the further away we are from being able to access our intuition.

The best way for me to describe this state is when it actually feels as if someone, or something else, is doing the actions. Athletes experience this as the 'zone', because they feel like they are not "doing" the running or jumping or throwing. The activity appears to be happening effortlessly.

As the bell curve begins to turn upward, (as happens when for example you are stressed or become overly attached to the results you are trying to produce) this is the precise moment when an emotion is triggered, moving you further away from your natural state. The more intense the state, the less intuition and control you have in managing situations.

**Emotional Intelligence Tools and Practice**

Maintaining your natural and most effective coaching state can be achieved using a variety of techniques.

Top of my list has to be the Sedona Method© founded by Lester Levenson and is now taught in Sedona, Arizona by Hale Dworskin through seminars, books and audio tapes. The striking simplicity of these techniques is almost beyond belief to many students and yet others have found it to be the most valuable methodology they have ever learned. (See our website for more details.)

The process is all about effortlessly letting go of unwanted thoughts, feelings and beliefs, in the same way you would drop a pen or pencil you were holding.

Persisting with this method undoubtedly improved my coaching and training techniques, because the moment my awareness tells me that my emotions and ego are beginning to kick in I instantly let go of those obstructing feelings and bring myself back to a place of complete openness and intuition.

Experience tells me that if I allow myself to become upset and emotional about a situation I stand less chance of reaching the desired outcome. I am sure you will remember having had an argument when you later realised that what was said in the heat of the moment was not only untrue, but had also prevented you from helping someone as much as you wanted to.

As a trainer, I have come across many challenging coaching situations. I remember a man, from London in his forties was having trouble deciding what he wanted out of life and who had become very upset.

His past as a gang member was severely haunting him and you can imagine how my heart began to race when he revealed that he had killed someone. Releasing and breathing allowed me to effectively and methodically work through these challenges. No judgement, just openness.

Once he realised no judgement was being made, he could relax, open his mind and tap into more of the great answers that were available to him. Now, 3 years later, he is a successful businessman and his commitment is to help youths avoid getting themselves into situations similar to his own.

This is an extreme and I am not suggesting that your coaching sessions will be like that, but I do know that your beliefs and values will be challenged and your ability to maintain your natural state is vital to enabling you to manage what can indeed be difficult situations.

It is interesting that when things go wrong we have a tendency to stop breathing! Regulating your breath will relax you and give you a moment or two to release and open again to the next question. Try to ensure that you are breathing abdominally and not drawing shallow breaths from your chest area.

Letting go of negative thoughts, beliefs and feelings can be so easy and even the deepest feelings and beliefs can be released if you have the willingness to simply let them go. This is where the Sedona Method comes into its own, by providing an extremely quick, practical and proven self-questioning, self-coaching technique to ground you.

You will discover that coachees who share your own values and beliefs are the easiest of people to coach, because you have complete and natural rapport. However, if you are to be successful as a coach the vital ingredient is that you are open to all coachees and "attached" to *none* of them.

**Strengthen your Beliefs as a Coach**

Presuppositions of NLP ( Neurolinguistic Programming ) are *convenient assumptions*, which you hold to be true without question and which, when integrated into your mindset as a coach, will accelerate performance.

Take a few moments now to take each of these presuppositions in turn and ask yourself how true you believe they really are. Allow yourself to acknowledge the possibility that they are true and review them on a regular basis to reinforce your belief system and strengthen your inner self as a coach.


**PROOF EXERCISE**

**Give three reasons why you know these to be true.**

*There is no such thing as failure – only feedback.*




*We respect each other's model of the world.*
*(How we view our experiences and how we perceive them).*

_All_ behaviour functions from positive intentions.

Everyone does the best they can with the resources they have.

The meaning of your communication lies in the response you get.

The person with the most flexibility of behaviour will control the system.

We are all in charge of our mind and therefore the result

*People are not their behaviours – accept the person for who they are and change their behaviour.*

*Resistance in someone is a sign of lack of rapport with him or her.*

*The map is not the territory*
   *I.e. the words we use are not the actual event or the item they represent.*

**Summary for Natural State**

Knowing that, in fact ,we are all capable of anything we put our minds to is fundamental to knowing to what level you can take your coaching ability.

What stops people from having what they want are the reasons they give as to why they can't have it. Letting go of these limitations frees the body and the subconscious mind to find the solution to any problem.

Realising that every limitation is self-inflicted, I take responsibility for my life and my results. By growing every day, I am learning to manage perceived difficult situations and, even more importantly, I have more control over my experience through life.

Avoid the temptation to blame outside circumstances for your problems. Develop your emotional intelligence consistently, because your ability to coach starts with mastering yourself.

## The three most important things to remember:

1. When you are in your natural state you will be more aware of what you need to do as a coach to get the results you and the coachee really want. You will instantly recognise when an approach is not working and immediately change that approach to produce the desired outcome.

2. Use the emotional intelligence model on a daily basis, to check your status in relation to that model at any moment in time; let go of any limiting thoughts, feelings and beliefs, thus bringing you back to your natural state as quickly as possible.

3. Strengthening the NLP presuppositions within yourself will improve your natural ability to coach and automatically create greater personal inner resourcefulness

# Chapter Three

The Enneagram
The most powerful Personal Development Tool for
consistently improving your Life and Performance as a
Coach

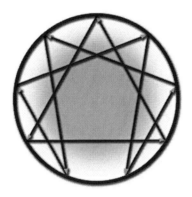

> *Depending on the circumstances,*
> *You should be as hard as a diamond,*
> *Flexible as a willow,*
> *Smooth flowing like water*
> *Or as empty as space*
>
> **Morihei Ueshiba**

## What is The Enneagram?

The Enneagram is one of the simplest and most practical of
profiling tools, which will provide a level of understanding about
yourself and others you have never had before.

The Enneagram is a geometric figure which maps out the nine fundamental personality types of human nature and their complex interrelationships. The descriptions of these nine types provides often astonishingly comprehensive understandings about the inner motivations, thought patterns, basic belief systems and emotional coping mechanisms of each one. Research suggests that the Enneagram type is established very early in childhood.

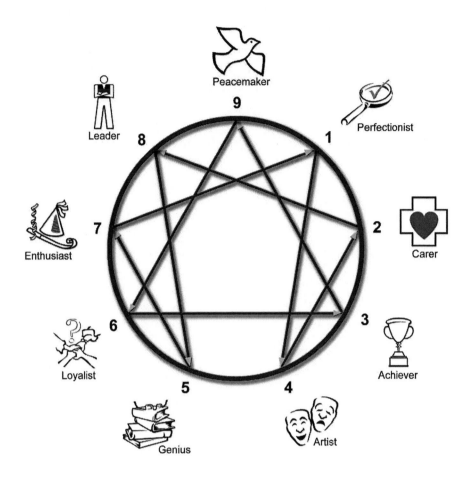

You will see how your Enneagram type amounts to something like a hypnotic trance. An understanding of the Enneagram will take you out of this trance and dramatically improve your productivity, results focus, and emotional intelligence by identifying the emotional and psychological traps you unwittingly set for yourself.

By highlighting your highest capacities and key strengths you will understand why some relationships work well for you and why others are not so easy.

You will become aware that if someone has responded badly to you in the past they are reacting from their hypnotic trance; so using this knowledge, if the same thing occurs again, there is no need to take things personally. As a coach, manager, parent or partner, the Enneagram can help to change the way you relate to others and also to understand the unconscious motivations underlying the way we operate.

Don Richard Riso and Russ Hudson provide one of the most valuable personal development resources in their book '**The**

**Wisdom of the Enneagram**'. (Bantam).

They give detailed insights into the history, makeup and applications of the Enneagram, together with breakdowns of each type, highlighting three ranges of behaviour from which we operate, depending on our level of emotional resistance and attachment to a situation, person or item.

Those of you familiar with Transactional Analysis will be aware of the three stages of behaviour known as Parent, Adult and Child. The Enneagram makes clear the different sets of behaviour patterns across three levels, which could easily correlate with Transactional Analysis principles.

The three levels are:

## UNHEALTHY

## AVERAGE

## HEALTHY

Once you have identified your own Enneagram type and become

familiar with the different levels of behaviour of that type, the resulting high level of self-awareness will signal when you need to change your approach to produce results through your coaching and indeed through life.

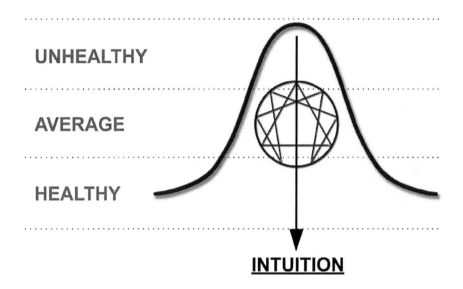

**INTUITION**

The extent to which a person is operating from the unhealthy aspect of their Enneagram profile, is in direct relationship to the extent to which they are 'identified' with the type or 'in trance', and unaware of the impact of their behaviour on others.

The more people are identified with their Enneagram type, the further away they are from being in their natural state and intuition. In your natural state you are far more 'aware' and can see through limiting patterns of behaviour,
permitting you to uncover more of the true potential within others and show them how to access these resources. In turn, they then can more effectively motivate and inspire themselves, even when the going gets a little rough.

In later chapters hints and tips are provided on how to identify your coachee's and team members' Enneagram types, together with suggestions for improving motivation.

The most important thing to remember is to always concentrate on your own development and appreciate the positive impact you create when you are relaxed and playful with your coaching. You will soon come to realise that it is in fact your own behaviour and intentions for your coachee which produces the results!

No Enneagram type makes a better coach than another. In fact, all of these types make excellent coaches when they are operating from the healthy aspect of their behaviour. The finest coaches and the ones who get great results consistently are those who are clearly operating from the healthy aspects of their Enneagram type.

Being aware of your own patterns mean you instinctively make better choices and access more of your natural state and intuition. Your increased emotional intelligence will equip you even better to handle difficult situations.

The more you know and work with the Enneagram, the more you will come to realise that people are not simply the sum of their behaviours and that actually we are capable of anything. With practice you will realise your own potential and discover that the potential within others is absolutely unlimited.

## The Enneagram Wings

Each type has a wing, sitting to one side of their core type on the diagram. So for example, a type six person will have a 7 or an 8 wing. This is why two people can have the same core type, yet their behaviour is somewhat different.

When you have identified your core type, refer to the Enneagram to identify your strongest wing. It does happen in some instances that a type can have strong tendencies pulled from both wings, but more often one wing will be dominant in their behaviour.

To know your wing type, read the descriptions either side of your core type and decide which one best describes you. On rare occasions a type can show some characteristics of both wings. Generally speaking, however, one wing appears much stronger.

For the purposes of this book, we will concentrate on your core type and show how you can use the Enneagram for coaching on a daily basis.

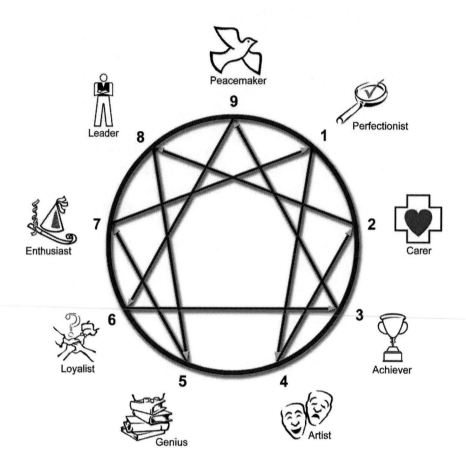

Peacemaker
9
Leader 8
Perfectionist
1
Enthusiast
7
2
Carer
Loyalist
6
3
Achiever
5
4
Genius
Artist

## Connected Types

The lines and arrows connecting the Enneagram types show what behaviours are likely to surface when operating from more extreme healthy and unhealthy positions.

So for example, when a Carer (2) feels uncomfortable as well as showing the unhealthy behaviour typical of a type 2 they also will begin to show behaviours of an unhealthy Boss (8) and yet when they are relaxed and operating from a healthy perspective they display the healthy characteristics of a 2 as well as some of the characteristics of an Artist (4).

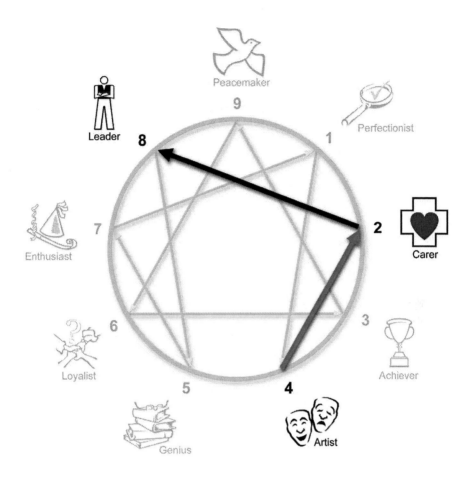

For a system as complex and comprehensive as the Enneagram, the above is necessarily a simplification. Nevertheless, it still yields very pertinent insights into the behaviour of people when they are having a so-called 'good day' or a 'bad day'.

**The decision-making Approaches of each Type**

The Enneagram can be divided into triads, grouping decision-making strategies and motivational drivers.

**Eights, Nines and Ones** are known as the **control triad** and people who fall into this section base much of their decision making on their gut instinct.

**Twos, Threes and Fours** are known as the **acceptance triad** and people who fall into this section base much of their decision

making on what their heart tells them.

**Fives, Sixes and Sevens** are known as the **security triad** and here people base much of their decision making on logic.

Being aware of the way you handle your own decision-making process can open up an exceptionally useful opportunity, if you are prepared to explore your intuition in greater depth. Useful because your intuition may well be telling you to make a less comfortable decision, but one which in fact turns out to be the right decision to make!

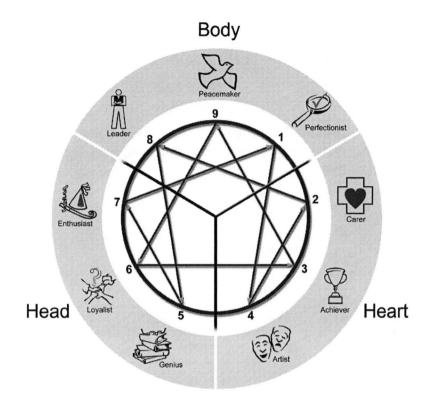

## The Three Wants of the Enneagram Types

Releasing negative emotions and thoughts when they arise has made such a difference to my coaching, especially in business. Watching yourself and the emotions that arise inside of you, then instantly letting go of them, will accelerate your coaching AND produce results. When a negative emotional response is triggered inside of us, it then generate one of three desires 'in the moment':

**Wanting Control**

**Wanting Acceptance or Approval**

**Wanting Security**

These 'wants' create emotional responses in the coach, making it harder to maintain a clear perspective of the appropriate coaching question which will change how the coachee feels and produce

results.

By letting go of the clutching feeling created by wanting control, your emotional state settles and actually gives you significantly *more* control. It is the same for wanting security and acceptance.

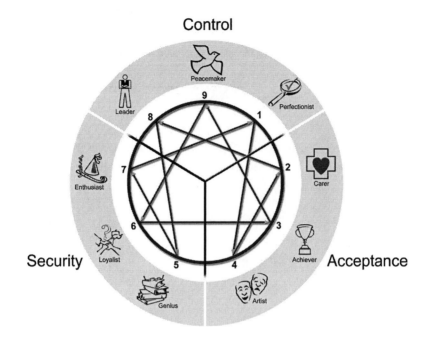

You probably know someone who wants to be liked so much that it actually makes you dislike them even more! Their wanting acceptance is in effect creating an emotional response taking them further away from their natural state and as such they meet with even less acceptance from others!

You can see from the Enneagram which of these three 'wants' each type has the tendency to experience and this forms part of their natural motivation.

Although, generally speaking, we all experience these wants to varying degrees, there are certain patterns which emerge:

**Eights, Nines, and Ones experience more wanting Control**

**Twos, Threes and Fours experience more wanting Acceptance**

**Fives, Sixes and Sevens experience more wanting Security**

Now, just imagine being a blank canvas:  no matter how much paint a person or situation throws at you ,none of it sticks – it all slides off, leaving the canvas perfectly clean.

Use this visualisation of a blank canvas to help you let go of all 'wants', leaving you with a clear and open perspective towards your coachee. Nothing that is said to you will be taken personally. Now, that is the state of mind from which your coaching can rise to a whole new level!

## The Enneagram Questionnaire – Discovering your Type

The following exercise has been designed to help you identify your Enneagram type.

Find somewhere quiet where you will not be disturbed. Take time to read through the following sets of behaviours and by using your gut feelings, intuition or logic, try and get a feel of which set you can relate to in terms of your everyday experience.

You may find that you can relate to more than one set of behaviours. If this is the case, then read the descriptions again and select the one that is MOST like you. As a last resort, ask someone close to you to review the types with you and give you their opinion as to your type.

Although we all share some of the characteristics of all nine types, our deepest motivations are driven by one core type which remains the same throughout our lives.

It is easier for people to identify profiles from the unhealthy aspects of their behaviour because they are more extreme. For this reason we have focused on more of these patterns.

Approach this exercise from a perspective of not having done any 'personal development' work and refer back to times when you were under considerable pressure. This will help you to identify your type more easily.

Should you still be uncertain as to your type at the end of this exercise and after reading more about the Enneagram, you can get confirmation by visiting our website and complete our more extensive on-line questionnaire that will provide you with a personalised report and a visual representation of the balance of behaviours across each of the nine types.

# The Enneagram Questionnaire

## TYPE A

I am strong willed and very independent.
I enjoy and instinctively take charge of situations
I am a straight talker and say what is on my mind without hesitation.
I can easily lose my temper but it quickly blows over and I soon forget it.
I am very happy to push people beyond their comfort zone.
I rise quickly to a challenge.
I will deny that I am tired or in pain.
I must be in control of my space and the people in my space.
Weak people can often irritate me.
I like people to be very direct with me.

When I am unhappy or uncomfortable I want to be on my own.
I have a very tender and loving side to me, but I rarely show it.
I make decisions easily
I have a tendency to overindulge in food and /or sex and /or alcohol.
I hate being controlled by others.
I have strong rules but am not afraid to break them.

## The Enneagram Questionnaire

# TYPE B

I like to be organised and structured
People perceive me as a serious person
I am very thorough and hate mistakes
I try to be honest and objective with myself
Before making a major purchase I will analyse everything first
I like rules and believe people should stick to them
I am happiest when I am physically active and having fun
I enjoy projects, particularly when a situation needs fixing. I can see immediately what needs to be done.
I sometimes pay a high price for trying to be perfect.
I am a good person.
I am hard on myself.
I am practical and realistic.
I am almost always on time.
It's either right or wrong and I know immediately whether something is right or wrong.
I have an internal critic that I cannot switch off.
I am a highly responsible person.

## The Enneagram Questionnaire

## TYPE C

I like to be different to everybody else.
I am very creative.
I cannot abide bad taste.
Generally I prefer to work on my own.
People hurt my feeling very easily.
I feel depressed for very long periods of time.
I hate not being understood
I like to contradict people and this makes people see me as being difficult.
I often feel that I am missing out on something.
I enjoy being unique
I am very attuned to me feelings.
I can easily empathise with other people's suffering
I am drawn towards things that are aesthetically pleasing and deeply touching or meaningful.
Authenticity is very important to me.

## The Enneagram Questionnaire

## TYPE D

I am very friendly.
I have a genuine concern for other people.
I always put other people's needs before my own.
I do not want to be dependant on other people.
It can be hard work looking after everyone else.
I believe that to get love you must give it.
I get a kick out of pleasing other people.
I hate not being appreciated for what I do.
People are more important then the result.
I like to make people feel comfortable.
I am attracted to mixing with important people.
I know how others are feeling and can adapt myself to behave the way they would like me to behave.
I don't like taking credit for things.
I think nothing of doing more for others than myself.

# The Enneagram Questionnaire

## TYPE E

I can easily see the advantage and disadvantage in every situation.
Unless I have a structure to my day I often get nothing done
I love to be with friends.
My focus tends to be on the demands of other people.
I try to please people.
I will do anything to avoid confrontation.
I see a part of me in each Enneagram type.
Peace and quiet is very important to me.
I often focus on activities that make me feel comfortable rather than what is important.
I very rarely show my anger.
It can be hard for me to know what I want.
I am very easy going
People perceive me as laid back.

## The Enneagram Questionnaire

# TYPE F

I am always busy doing something.
I have a positive attitude.
I think nothing of working overtime.
I can be very impatient.
I believe it is important to get things done quickly.
I will do anything to avoid failure.
I am enthusiastic and enjoy leadership roles.
I feel my emotions often distract me from getting things done.
I love competition.
I hate people who are indecisive and /or inefficient.
I thrive on prestige and power.
I believe people are rewarded for what they do and not just for being who they really are.
I like the best of everything.
I am often criticised for pushing people too hard.
I like to look good.
I find it easy to inspire people.

# The Enneagram Questionnaire

## TYPE G

I love being part of a team
I am always questioning things.
I am very supportive of people.
I would find it very difficult to trust someone again if they broke my trust.
I often use humour, wit and sarcasm.
I can be very hard working.
I operate more effectively when I know I am completely safe.
I believe the world is a dangerous place.
I am very good at solving problems and puzzles.
I can be very emotional although I don't often show it.
I often find myself questioning peoples' motives.
I can be sceptical and look for problems.
I fear being on my own.
If I am honest with myself, I prefer not to take a leadership role.
I can be a very anxious person.
I find myself always wondering what will go wrong.

## The Enneagram Questionnaire

## TYPE H

I love to do a variety of things and if I don't I tend to get bored very quickly.
I love excitement and travel.
I like to organise parties and social events.
I am quite happy to say what is on my mind but sometimes it gets me into trouble.
I like upbeat people.
I am playful and optimistic.
I have a very good imagination.
I make a commitment but then soon feel trapped by it.
People say I look a lot younger than I am.
I like trying new and interesting things.
I cannot stand being bored.
Sometimes it feels like I am thinking of 12 things or more at the same time .
I am easily distracted.

# The Enneagram Questionnaire

## TYPE I

I am a very private person.
I consider myself an expert in one or two areas.
I like to know all there is to know about a subject I am interested in.
I hate people making demands on me.
I spend a great deal of time on my own.
I can keep very calm in a crisis.
I go out of my way to avoid loud and offensive people.
People perceive me as a shy person.
I love reading, in fact I prefer to study a subject as opposed to practice it.
I am very sensitive to criticism.
I sometimes find it hard to communicate effectively with people.
Some people see me as negative.

The following list of types will point you in the direction of your Enneagram type.

A -     8 THE LEADER
B -     1 THE PERFECTIONIST
C -     4 THE ARTIST
D -     2 THE CARER
E -     9 THE PEACEMAKER
F -     3 THE ACHIEVER
G -     6 THE LOYALIST
H -     7 THE ADVENTURER
I -     5 THE GENIUS

 (1) - **The Perfectionist.**

Wants to do things properly and get it right. Is honest and responsible.
An eye for detail!

 (2) - **The Carer.**

Wants to help other people to meet their needs and wants.
Looks after others!

(3) - **The Achiever.**

Wants to work hard to be the best and to be admired for what they have achieved.
Going for gold!

(4) – **The Artist.**

Wants to be unique, genuine and different.
Life is a drama!

(5) – **The Genius.**

Wants to amass knowledge and information, to feel safe in his/her own world.
Expert in his or her own field!

(6) – **The Loyalist**

Wants to be part of a team as well as able to trust in them self and others.
Team player and questioner!

 (7) – **The Enthusiast**

Wants to live life to the full by exploring a multiplicity of experiences.
Fun, fun, fun!

 (8) – **The Leader**

Wants to be assertive, in full control and protect those perceived to be defenceless.
Always in charge!

## (9) – The Peacemaker

Wants to merge with others' agendas, keep the peace, and be part of the whole rather than stand out. As such they often relate to characteristics of all nine types.
Live and Let Live!

## Summary for the Enneagram

### Three Key Things to remember about the Enneagram:

1. Identify your core Enneagram type and study the three levels of behaviour: Healthy....... Average.......... Unhealthy.
2. You are much more than your Enneagram type. Taking yourself out of trance allows you access your natural state and understand the impact your behaviours, thoughts and feelings have on every situation and each coaching interaction.
3. Concentrate on your own behaviour in relation to the Enneagram
   before using it to coach others.

# Chapter Four

# How to accelerate and improve your Performance as a Coach using the Enneagram?

*Watch your thoughts; they become words.*
*Watch your words; they become actions.*
*Watch your actions; they become habits.*
*Watch your habits; they become character.*
*Watch your character; it becomes your destiny.*

**--Frank Outlaw**

By now you should have identified your type.
In this chapter you will find:

1. Overviews of the types.
2. Names of famous people and possible career preferences relating to each type.
3. Details of what to look for in terms of the Healthy, Average and Unhealthy behaviours.
4. A description of the types in a coaching role.
5. Exercises to develop healthy behaviour patterns.

The key to using this section is to take the information seriously-lightly and just enjoying noticing your behaviour in different situations. Make a mental note of the different results you get from others, through using your awareness of their Enneagram type.

In this book we focus on how the Enneagram can help you with your coaching, but you will find that it does in fact impact across all areas of your life.

I recommend you read the descriptions in the following order:

1. Your core type
2. The type you move towards when you are at your worst (des-integration)
3. The type you move towards when at your very best (integration)
4. Your wing type

Moving from unhealthy to healthy behaviour happens in an instant, when you know who you are at your very best and you begin to practice focusing purely on your natural strengths. After all, why bother with any other behaviour than you at your best!!

The Proof Exercises will accelerate your development and I recommend doing a minimum of one each week. Use only the exercises for your core and wing types. For the time being, leave all other exercises alone.

Journal your developments on a daily basis to help you integrate the learning even more quickly.

## THE PERFECTIONIST

> "I'd rather be right than President"
>
> **John C.Calhoun**

| | |
|---|---|
| **Also known as:** | Reformer, Judge, Purist, Humanitarian, Teacher |
| **World View:** | Always do the right thing<br>Let me teach you |
| **Focus on:** | What's out of place?<br>What's right or wrong in any situation?<br>What needs to be improved?<br>Life is about continually working towards a set of high internal standards. |
| **Basic Fear:** | Being wrong |
| **Virtues:** | Patience |
| **Natural Coaching and Leadership Style:** | Visionary, structured, committed, lead by example, spontaneous, considers many possibilities rather than one right way. |

## Overview Of The Perfectionist (ONES)

**ONES** are known for their strong sense of responsibility, which drives their need to improve the world, 'get things right', and strive for excellence in all they do.

**ONES** feel a sense of mission in their life. Their high standards and ideals often lead them to positions of power in organisations. They have an intuitive sense of what is, or could be, right in a

certain situation and how it can be improved.

They desire their work to be a mirror of their own very high standards and are attracted to others with equally high values. They focus on doing their best and encouraging others to realise their full potential, with a view to making the world a better place for all.

**ONES** see themselves as honest, objective, reliable, ethical and self-disciplined. They are motivated by the need to be right. They themselves don't like to be criticised and will do all they can to avoid criticism.

They are superb critical thinkers and can spend a great deal of time thinking about the consequences of their actions. They think of themselves as taking a logical approach to situations when they are, in fact, being driven by a strong internal sense that it is something they must do.

On occasions, people may feel as though they are being overly criticized or rejected if the Perfectionist is constantly nit-picking, demanding perfection or sermonizing.

Feelings of resentment surface towards those they see as flouting 'the rules' and getting away with it, although they try not to show these feelings openly because it 'wouldn't be right'.

Healthy aspects of the personality develop when **ONES** begin to balance their desire to maintain absolute standards with a compassion for the opinions and feelings of others. They become less judgemental of themselves and others and spend time building

relationships. They are then much more forgiving of mistakes.

### Famous ONES

Mary Whitehouse
Hilary Clinton
Nelson Mandela
Margaret Thatcher
Pope John Paul II
Iain Paisley
Mahatma Ghandi
Cherie Blair
Mary Poppins
Celine Dion
Katherine Hepburn
Harrison Ford
Nicole Kidman

### Possible Career Preferences

Lawyers
Politicians
Management Roles
Precision Engineers
Church Leaders
Accountants
Project Management
Teachers

### ONE-TYPE Organisation

Motorola

## Connected Types

Healthy – **ONES** take on some of the characteristics of **SEVENS** (Enthusiast)
Unhealthy – **ONES** take on some of the characteristics of **FOURS** (Artist)

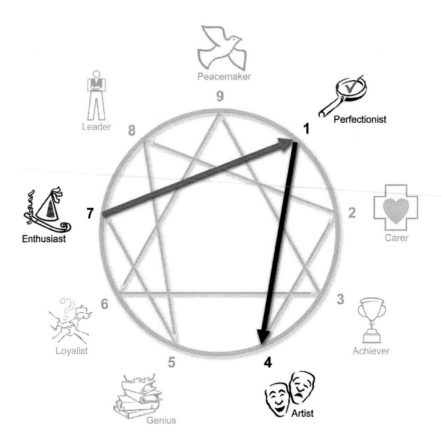

**Healthy**

Open and accepting of mistakes
Light-hearted and having fun
Active as they naturally move towards the healthy aspect of a 'type 7' - Adventurer
Enthusiastic, caring and supportive of themselves and others
Focus more on the positive points of performance.
Trust that other people <u>may</u> know the right way of achieving things.
Expressive in their appreciation for others and their efforts regularly
Full acceptance of their weaker points
Committed in their quest to achieve results
Highly visionary, able to provide positive direction to others


**Average**

Debate the validity of someone else's viewpoint.
Too methodical in their approach
Correct people for mistakes they have made and judgemental of their behaviour.
Direct people instead of allowing them take responsibility.
Inflexible.
Pent-up anger and frustration through worrying.

**Unhealthy**

Use of sarcasm and cynicism
Uncompromising.
Controlling of others.
Become inwardly angry with themselves and others.
They lose trust in people.
Being defensive.
Constant longing for good results from people
Highly-strung and emotional showing characteristics of a 'type 4'.
Develop physical ailments such as arthritis and back pain from holding too much tension in the body.

**The Perfectionist Coach**
**Meet Sarah – Senior Manager**

Sara has been Senior Manager for a large finance company for 2 years. Always dressed in crisp, smart attire, she shows high levels of commitment on a daily basis. In fact, she has rarely taken a day off sick.

Results Coaching in 60 Seconds provided Sara with a structure with which she could learn and apply coaching easily. She understands the rules of coaching and sticks to the three primary rules with every coaching interaction.

1. Being in her natural state
2. Having a clear outcome/objective
3. Using one or more steps to move people towards the desired result

Well-balanced, fair, honest and helpful towards others, she gives people clear direction and uses her coaching skills and natural

desire for improvement to motivate and inspire others.

She worked hard to let go of her 'inner critic' that would, at first, frequently point out to her what she was doing wrong. This releasing process actually increased her efficiency as she learned to drop negative thoughts about herself as they arose, allowing her to focus on excellence rather than perfection.

When at her best she is playful with members of her team and approaches coaching lightly and with a sense of humour. Through this training and awareness she has learned to be spontaneous and flexible with her coaching and relax more when things do not go according to plan.

Collaborative in her approach to coaching, she is now more accepting of mistakes made by herself and others. She uses laughter to release pent-up frustration in the moment, bringing herself more into her natural state when feeling under pressure.

Occasionally her attention is too directed towards what is 'wrong'. When she senses that people see her as nit picking she explains that she is only trying to help. This helps her not only to defuse a situation but also to refocus herself and the people she is coaching on excellence rather than perfection. She has also found that taking a 'what if…' approach to her questioning inspires more creativity in herself and others.

Taking regular 5-minute breaks during the day and spending time relaxing and taking physical exercise in the evening naturally diffuses any pent-up emotion. It leaves her feeling more open when she goes to bed and therefore fully relaxed when she awakes - ready to start each day feeling happy and energised.

## THE PERFECTIONIST

### PROOF EXERCISES

Take very small, regular five-minute breaks during the day to de-stress. It is important that you clear any unwanted stress from a previous coaching scenario before moving on to the next.

Accentuate your fun and enthusiastic side through your coaching. People love being made to laugh and by opening them up to your coaching they are far more receptive.

Combine being spontaneous with your coaching and also using planned coaching sessions. Learn to be flexible with your coaching.

Ask someone whom you spend time with and trust to remind you to take it easy on yourself. Explain to them what you are learning about yourself and ask them for support.

Review people's behaviour from the past few days and practice forgiving and accepting the mistakes they have made. Remind yourself of their perfections rather than the imperfections.

Allow people to make their own decisions. You will generate more self-esteem for them, even if you strongly believe that your ideas provide the right solutions.

When coaching, only offer your solutions as an absolute last resort and even then make sure you have their genuine agreement on taking advice from you.

Take regular exercise and create some time to allow yourself to relax. Remember you love being active and it helps you to release unwanted, pent-up anger.

## THE CARER

*"You can have everything you want in life if you help others get what they want."*

**Zig Ziglar**

| | |
|---|---|
| **Also known as:** | Helper, Giver, Guardian Angel, The Lover, Altruist |
| **World View:** | I support and help others. |
| **Focus on:** | How to bring out the best in others. |
| **Basic Fear:** | Of not being liked or loved |
| **Virtues:** | Humility |
| **Natural Coaching and Leadership Style:** | Cheerleaders, enthusiastic encouragement, unconditionally supportive, servant leader. |

### Overview of the Carer

**TWOS** are known for their genuine desire to unconditionally help, love and support others with patience and compassion and with a desire to bring out the best in them. They are incredibly attuned to the needs and wants of others on a moment-to-moment basis.

When that help is conditional, however, it stems from a need to be needed, from a growing unawareness of their own needs (or a belief that they have none) and an inability to say no to others' requests and demands.

There may be a desire to seduce, manipulate and to flatter others to get their approval. They begin to invest much more in relationships in which they themselves feel wanted and needed.

Healthy aspects of the personality develop when **TWOS** realise the importance of meeting their own needs themselves, and begin to accept unconditional help from others.

Compassionate and humane, **TWOS** value people and are concerned for others' well being. They prefer to manage people one at a time, in order to provide focus on individual needs. They like to be appreciated and as such are proactive in praising people and making them feel important. Often perceived as being the power behind the throne, **TWOS** can be ambitious and dedicated to helping people in positions of power to succeed.

| **Famous TWOS** | **Possible Career Preferences** |
|---|---|
| Mother Theresa | Nurse |
| Tony Blair | Personal Assistant |
| Desmond Tutu | Counsellor |
| Nancy Reagan | Therapist |
| John Travolta | Housewife |
| Elvis Presley | Nursery teachers |
| Snow White | |
| Florence Nightingale | **TWO Organisation** |
| Sally Jessy Raphael | |
| Mary Kay Ash | UK National Health Service |
| Bill Cosby | RSPCA |
| Melanie Griffith | |
| Monica Lewinsky | |

## Connected Types

Healthy – **TWOS** take on some of the characteristics of **FOURS** (Artist)
Unhealthy –**TWOS** take on some of the characteristics of **EIGHTS** (Leaders)

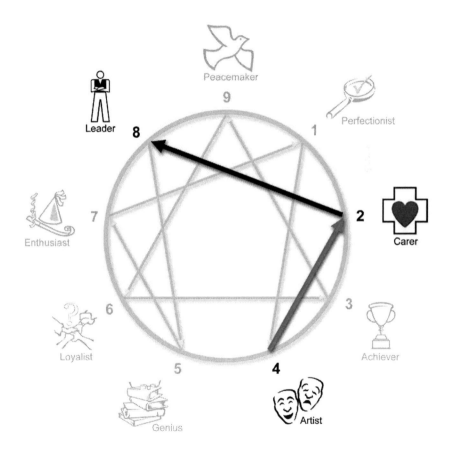

## Healthy

Unconditionally supportive to the person they are coaching.
Approach coaching without any expectation
Show genuine enthusiasm for others.
Adaptable.
Friendly and sensitive
Maintain empathy and maintain their viewpoint
Masters of identifying the true needs of others
They allow people to ask for help rather than constantly offering it.

## Average

Using flattery to win people over.
Lay claim to other people's achievements.
Become angry at the often-false belief that other people are taking them for granted.
Draw attention to their good deeds for others.
Not letting the people they are coaching follow through on their own.
Offer coaching whether someone needs it or not
Compulsive giving.
People pleasing.

## Unhealthy

Playing the role of the martyr.

Demanding that people repay them for what they have done for them.

Having lost sense of self they begin to exaggerate their contributions and self-importance and become very prideful

Become desperate to be liked and loved be people.

Manipulating.

Hysterical.

## The Carer Coach- Meet Jane – Business Manager

Jane works as Business Manager for a sales company. Responsible for the performance of 12 Sales Managers, Jane speaks personally to each and goes out of her way to coach them every day.

Her continual sensitivity and desire to assist them in doing their job well and getting the results they want occasionally leads to neediness and feelings of "they cannot do this without me". Her new awareness of the Enneagram reminds her to let go of her attachment to being needed, and the desire to give just to get. She can begin to focus on her own responsibilities as well as those of others.

Being so externally focused on the needs of others makes her a wonderful coach. She unconditionally helps them with genuine enthusiasm, and shows appreciation for their efforts. This naturally builds self-esteem in others.

Occasionally, Jane forgets that in order for her coaching to be successful her support must be given unconditionally and not to use coaching to manipulate results for her own gain.

Sometimes she feels that others should be giving more back to her, maybe in terms of commitment, forgetting for a moment that they operate from a different set of internal rules and beliefs about the need to give.

She now allows Bob to coach her on a daily basis. The idea is to encourage her to receiving coaching herself, without having to feel that she has to offer help in return, (something **TWOS** often find hard to do). She pays close attention to herself during a coaching session and to any desire to turn the conversation around so that the attention is away from her and on Bob.

Her understanding of the Enneagram takes away the judgement

she used to have about people and their behaviours, allowing her to focus on her own approach to coaching. She has become very aware of the impact her own behaviour has on others' performance.

Accessing her natural state by relaxing and emotionally detaching herself from other people's problems gives her a clearer perspective. It allows her to access more of her intuition, as opposed to making assumptions about what the person is feeling and what they need to do. It also allows her to engender more responsibility and focus on improving performance, rather than to listening to people's stories.

Her humanistic management style now shines through consistently, because she realises that an aggressive approach to management simply indicates that she is under pressure and operating from the unhealthy aspects of her profile.

She finds it relatively easy to let go of her feelings and negative thoughts and now ensures she daily spends a minimum of one hour in her own company, giving herself the attention she too deserves.

 **THE CARER**

## PROOF EXERCISES

Go through an entire day not caring what other people think about you. You maybe surprised to find people like you more for it!

The next time someone offers you something, take it gratefully without giving anything in return. Allow them to enjoy giving to you.

Create boundaries for yourself that prevent you from becoming entangled with other people's negative emotions. To be successful you need to develop a strong emotional detachment, to offer a clear perspective as a coach.

In coaching and management situations, know exactly what you want and make your position perfectly clear to the people you are working with.

Notice the tendency to use flattery to gain others' approval and instead sparingly use genuine compliments.

Learn to distinguish between other people's needs and your own and make sure you create a healthy balance between the two. Make sure you receive regular coaching yourself.

If you feel someone you are coaching is taking advantage of you in a coaching situation, stay calm and immediately express how you feel. Maybe they are taking too much of your time? Are you allowing them to become dependent on you?

Your family and children – learn to develop interests of your own, it will prevent you from worrying unnecessarily about them.

# *THE ACHIEVER*

> *"I wasn't afraid to fail.*
> *Something good always comes out of failure."*
>
> **Anne Baxter**

| | |
|---|---|
| **Also known as:** | The Performer, the Motivator, the Producer |
| **World View:** | Life is a competition, success is judged by your achievements |
| **Focus on:** | Setting goals and doing whatever it takes to achieve them |
| **Basic Fear:** | Failure |
| **Virtues:** | Honesty |
| **Natural Coaching and Leadership Style:** | Task orientated, enthusiastic, |

## Overview Of The Achiever

Enthusiastic and highly efficient, **THREES** have an incredible drive to succeed and produce results. Achievers like to be responsible for their own output and work very quickly indeed. In business they always keep the market in mind and love to work with strategy planning designed to produces results fast.

They shine in the workplace because they are naturally driven to make things 'work'. Self-starters, **THREES** are happy taking risks; the danger comes when they cut corners to produce results that cost them dearly later. Their core motivation is that success will

bring them praise and positive attention from others.

**THREES** like being noticed for their accomplishments and know what it takes to make things happen. Superb at focusing on the task in hand, **THREES** want to win and believe they can do anything they set their mind to.

Having an infectious energy, **THREES** can effortlessly motivate and inspire others to do well always focusing on solutions and not problems. At times their approach to a task is so fast that they leave their colleagues behind.

Putting their feelings to one side, they have a tendency to rush into activity that they believe will generate more recognition and reward, sometimes forgetting what they really want or what their real feelings are.

Dressed for success they focus on their self-image to make a good impression with people. The desire for social status, fear of failure and an attempt to protect self-image often leads to them cutting corners, which could have long-term consequences.

Healthy aspects of the personality develop when integrity is not sacrificed in the name of success, and they allow their 'unpackaged' true nature to come through.

| Famous THREES | Possible Career Preferences |
|---|---|
| Jeffrey Archer | |
| Victoria Beckham | Sales Roles |
| Oprah Winfrey | Sports |
| Paul McCartney | Executives |
| Tom Cruise | Businesspeople |
| George Clooney | Fashion Models |
| Uri Geller | Celebrities |
| Greg Rusedski | Actors/actresses |
| Geri Halliwell | |
| Val Kilmer | **THREE Organisations** |
| Tiger Woods | |
| Dan Quayle | McDonalds |
| | FedEx |

**Connected Types**

Healthy –**THREES** take on some of the characteristics of **SIXES** (Loyalists)
Unhealthy –**THREES** take on some of the characteristics of **NINES** (Peacemakers

## Healthy

They accept themselves for who they are without seeking approval from others.
Very aware of other people's values and take them into account when coaching to motivate and inspire them
Kind to others and allow them to take full credit for their achievements.
Focused at setting goals and persisting with them until they are achieved.
Self-motivating.
Exhibit natural flair for leadership and take into account what is best for the entire team.

## Average

Cut corners to maintain their image.
Workaholics.
Create an attractive and positive image for themselves to cover self-doubt as to who they think they should be.
Fear of failure and having other people not notice them.

## Unhealthy

Self-deception using dishonest strategies to manipulate situation to their advantage and create an impression that they are successful
Plan and implement revenge attacks towards people that have let

them down or whom they fear.
Experience problems when making decisions.
Become vindictive towards others.
Self-centred
Superficial and pretentious

## The Achiever Coach

### Meet Andrew – Sales Manager for a Computer Company.

Highly motivated and an ex-sales person himself, Andrew is responsible for a team of 12 sales people. Often working 16 hours or more each day is not uncommon for Andrew and in that time he rarely takes a break.

His emotional intelligence is now greater than ever before. He pays full attention to any feelings of fear of failure and instead of putting them to one side uses them as a signal to slow down and think things through before rushing forward.

Taking time to get to know people has been of enormous benefit. Over the past few months he has changed his approach to managing his team and now adopts an inter-dependant style. Rather than focusing on his own sales contribution, he concentrates on developing his team to deliver increased sales as a unit.

Reading the Enneagram he suddenly realised that not everyone has the same drive for success and nor should they. Being so motivated himself to produce results, he would often wonder why others were not equally so inclined. Consequently he has been far more flexible in the demands he makes on his team, and quickly realises when he is being unrealistic.

Slowing down has been a difficult lesson for him, but Andrew now provides clearer and more considerate feedback and coaching. This approach is bringing out the very best of his motivational skills and focusing people on specific sales results. "It's ironic that taking more time actually makes myself and the team even more productive – I would never have believed it before."

Andrew has learned to pay attention to his feelings and those of others and use them when coaching, rather than think that feelings get in the way of good performance. This approach guarantees that people feel comfortable and driven to produce results. It replaces the old method of saying – "just do it!"

In the past he would regularly 'take over' situations that were perhaps not working for people, instead of coaching them to handle the situation themselves.

He now rarely takes the credit for a good performance within his team and finds that his team respond better. They receive full recognition for their efforts and frequently attract the attention of Senior Managers in the organisation.

## THE ACHIEVER

## **PROOF EXERCISES**

When coaching, allow yourself time. Slow down. Remember that not all people are used to processing information as quickly as you do and you need to coach at a pace which is comfortable for the person you are coaching. This way you will be even more inspiring to people and they will be more committed to working with you.

Be aware when you are projecting an image, as opposed to just being yourself. When you are coaching, people must feel they can trust you and if they cannot do so, they will not be relaxed enough to truly perform at their best. Remember, an athlete performs best when he or she is most relaxed and focused.

Practice honesty. Note your tendency to lie, just to get a result. Even if you win the rat race – you are still a rat! People must trust you if you are to consistently produce a good performance through them.

Practice meditation. You will learn to handle your emotions effectively, so that rather than pushing them aside you will free tremendous energy to achieve even more. Practice letting go of any fear of failure.

Make time for team members on a daily basis. Spend a few moments with each of them building and developing strong relationships.

Take regular holidays and leave ALL your work at home!

## THE ARTIST

*"Each morning when I awake, I experience again a supreme pleasure - that of being Salvador Dali"*

**Salvador Dali**

| | |
|---|---|
| **Also known as:** | Actor, Actress, Romantic, Individualist, Creator, The Victim |
| **World View:** | I am authentic. Something seems to be missing. If only things were different. The never-ending search for the longed-for things that are missing, to make life complete |
| **Focus on:** | What makes me stand out from the crowd? How can I be different and unique? |
| **Basic Fear:** | Of being without consistent personal identity, abandonment, rejection, loss, not being special. |
| **Virtues:** | Melancholy |
| **Natural Coaching and Leadership Style:** | Impulsive and passionate, inspire others to new depths of being authentic |

## Overview of the Artist

**FOURS** are known for their idealism, creativity, sensitivity and appreciation of all things beautiful and aesthetically pleasing.

Their basic desire is to be unique, authentic and original and consequently they search for the deeper meaning of experiences.

Highly intuitive and completely in touch with their own feelings, **FOURS** naturally show strong empathy with the suffering of others, which can sometimes prevent them from handling situations effectively.

Their clothing and personal space reflects their desire to be different and special and can often make them appear aloof and elitist to others. They experience strong feelings of melancholy regarding what is missing in their life.

Healthy aspects of the personality develop when their sensitivity to feelings is balanced by a rational acceptance of the need to attend to the positive and good aspects of their lives right now, instead of continually feeling into the past or future for what was or could be better.

| Famous FOURS | Possible Career Preferences |
|---|---|
| Marlon Brando | |
| Gwyneth Paltrow | Actor/Actress |
| Judy Garland | Connoisseur |
| The Artist (Formerly known as | Singer |
| Prince) | Stage and Theatre |
| Michael Jackson | Entertainer |
| James Dean | Artist |
| Vincent Van Gogh | |
| Salvador Dali | |
| Elizabeth Taylor | |

**FOUR**
**Organisations**

Harrods
Tiffany's
Ritz Carlton
Thorntons

## Connected Types

Healthy – **FOURS** take on some of the characteristics of **ONES** (Perfectionist)
Unhealthy – **FOURS** take on some of the characteristics of **TWOS** (Carers)

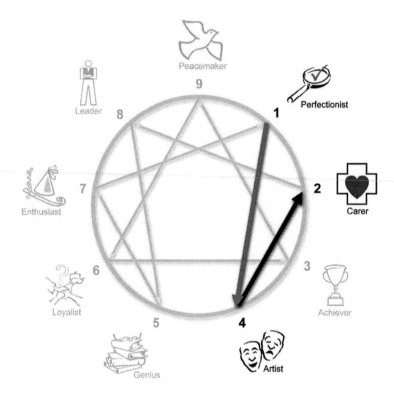

## Healthy

Very creative indeed allowing others to expand their awareness
Being sensitive to others' needs
Wonderfully articulate
Highly creative and perceptive
Individual style of coaching
Empathetic and intuitive
Genuinely compassionate.

## Average

Turn inward and daydream about what might be.
Become envious of the people they are coaching.
Are melodramatic with people.
Have a constant feeling that they are missing out on something
Worry that others do not appreciate them.

## Unhealthy

Envious
Depression
Self-sabotage and sabotage of others.
Self-absorbed
Temperamental
Masochistic and extravagant
Critical of others
Absorbed in their feelings, particularly guilt

**The Artist Coach**

**Julie – Senior Manager**

Highly creative and able to hold a strong vision for herself and indeed the organisation, Julie intentionally chose a career that would allow her to use her creative skills on a daily basis. She now coaches newer member of the team to inspire creativity in them.

Realising that her resistance to completing the more mundane activities comes from her Enneagram pattern, she make more effort to help the team complete the more routine, but necessary daily tasks.

As with all **FOURS**, Julie is very aware of her feelings. She uses this awareness to overcome her fears when coaching anyone she perceives as more creative than herself. This releases any feelings of envy and produces better results for both her and her team.

The degree to which Julie is effective and efficient often is a direct reflection of her current emotional state; emotions take precedence and the objective becomes irrelevant. Continued emotional intelligence development, using Sedona method techniques, allows Julie to manage these emotions, both for her own good and that of others around her.

Instead of appreciating what is good and pleasant now, Julie tends instead to look for what's missing, and to imagine what could be better tomorrow or what was better yesterday.

Julie's introspection and sensitivity produces great empathy with others and the ability to help and support them closely.

Excessive introspection, however, leads to feelings of isolation, envy, longing and wallowing in melancholy.

Overall, her natural creativity is instrumental in drawing out the same quality in others. She encourages people to consider different ways of approaching the most mundane of objectives, bringing greater enjoyment to the process.

# THE ARTIST

## PROOF EXERCISES

Beware of misreading other people's feelings about you. Pay attention to what is actually said, rather than mistaking feelings triggered by old relationships that could fool you into believing the worst.

Acknowledge the possibility that someone else may be better than you at doing certain tasks, and learn to truly admire him or her for it. Allow yourself and others to appreciate who they are right now.

Work closely with people you trust and ask them to give you personal feedback on a regular basis.

Keep your own problems and issues to yourself when coaching others. Be completely open to their needs and focus on coaching them to improve their situation and not yours.

Notice the tendency to feeling envious of other people's success. A great coach will want their people to be successful and are open to others being better then they are at certain activities.

Practice observing your feelings without getting caught up in them. It will give you a clearer perspective and keep your creativity channels open, especially in difficult situations.

# THE GENIUS

> *"Science without religion is lame, religion without science is blind"*
>
> **Albert Einstein**

| | |
|---|---|
| **Also known as:** | The Thinker, The Sage, The Guru, The Philosopher |
| **World View:** | I am the master of my private world<br>I am committed to being an expert and master in my chosen field |
| **Focus on:** | Intellectual Firepower |
| **Basic Fear:** | Of being useless |
| **Virtues:** | Non-attachment |
| **Natural Coaching and Leadership Style:** | Ambitious and in pursuit of control<br>Masters of their field. |

## Overview of The Genius

**FIVES** are known for their detailed knowledge of their subject matter, their wisdom, their genius, their ability to synthesise knowledge in a new way, their privacy, their emotional detachment and calmness in times of crisis.

**FIVES** seek safety in gaining knowledge. There is a strong desire to learn all there is to learn about a particular subject. They are very analytical, objective, and detailed in their planning and thinking. They have a gift for being able to simply, logically and rationally explain their ideas and theories. They are driven by the desire to understand why things are the way they are.

Attention is directed toward the unusual and unfamiliar in the hope that their specialist area is not conventional and others will not come to know more than they do about their field of expertise. Intense focus can lead to making remarkable discoveries and creating inventions that change the world.

The emotional detachment extends to their personal life, where they are more comfortable sharing ideas, plans, facts and figures rather than feelings. They dislike intrusions in their life, and would rather spend time alone than in a group.

Healthy aspects of the personality develop when **FIVES** take time out to experience their feelings instead of retreating into thinking all the time.

Rarely communicating with people, **FIVES** likes to be independent and in total control of their time and space. To achieve this they can spend much time alone.

Their ability to move towards the healthy aspects of type **EIGHT** can make them terrific coaches when they fully understand and are confident with the processes of coaching.

## Famous FIVES

Bill Gates
Richard Bandler
Albert Einstein
Anthony Hopkins
Stephen King
Stephen Hawking
Thomas Edison
Warren Buffet
Sinead O'Connor

## Possible Career Preferences

Scientist
Research
Computers
Technical Services
Chemist

## FIVE Organisation

C-Span
(Objective News Gathering
Company)

## Connected Types

Healthy – **FIVES** take on some of the characteristics of **EIGHTS** (Leaders)
  Unhealthy – **FIVES** take on some of the characteristics of **SEVENS** (Enthusiasts)

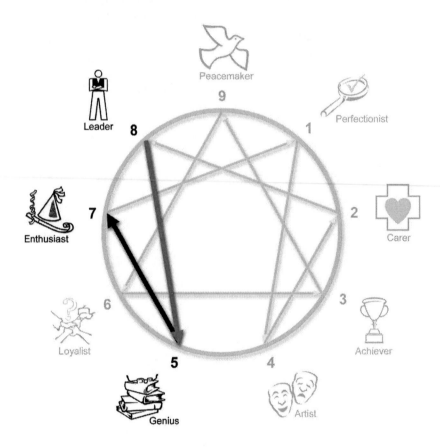

**Healthy**

Clear-minded and compassionate
Confident in themselves
Inventive
Kind and open-minded
Perceptive
Completely trustworthy
Highly objective

**Average**

Continuously studying
Resentful of others' confidence
Spend more time alone
Scornful towards people who do not understand them
Demanding
Know-it-all in attitude
Detachment and withdrawal

**Unhealthy**

Cut themselves off from the outside world
Over-active mind chatter
A desire to escape from reality
Intolerant

**The Genius Coach**
**Meet John – Senior Director of a Computer Software Company**

John has a wider and all-encompassing knowledge of his company's software programmes than anyone else within the company. He is highly confident in his own skills and abilities to write any software programme when asked. He brings this same approach to the in-depth study of coaching processes, before applying many of the tools with his team.

He has, in fact, taken such a deep interest that he spends hours studying coaching principles in his spare time.

He adopts a detached, observational stance when coaching, which sometimes appears introvert but serves him well when working with more emotional types.

Taking physical exercise at his local fitness centre John has benefited from becoming more in touch with his feelings which has given him more balance between his logical mind and his intuition. He now notices and pays attention to his emotions and the emotions of others. He uses this awareness more to support people in using feelings as a resource to produce results.

Unexpected confrontations and tricky situations can sometimes cause disproportionate fear. But by practicing using his connected **EIGHT** qualities, John is learning to handle the most difficult of coaching situations very effectively indeed by taking more control of every interaction.

**THE GENIUS**

**<u>PROOF EXERCISES</u>**

Consider doing physical activity on a regular basis to develop your feeling senses and increase your energy levels. It will raise awareness of both your own feelings and those of others; vital to knowing when a person feels motivated to follow through with agreed actions.

Take risks and speak up in front of people. Be confident in sharing your insights with others.

Understand you do not have to know everything about coaching to be good at it. Allow yourself to practice the theories and principles you are learning, to improve your knowledge even more through experience.

Spend 15 minutes each day developing your communication skills and building confidence in talking and being with people.

Put yourself in a situation you perceive as being difficult to handle and note that dealing with it is often nowhere near as bad as you 'think' it is going to be.

# *THE LOYALIST*

> *"Damned if you do.*
> *Damned if you don't."*

| | |
|---|---|
| **Also known as:** | Team Player, Loyal Sceptic, Devils Advocate, The Trouble-Shooter, The Questioner |
| **World View:** | The world is a dangerous place<br>I need to be able to trust you |
| **Focus on:** | Making things safe |
| **Basic Fear:** | Having no support<br>Not being able to survive on their own |
| **Virtues:** | Courage |
| **Natural Coaching and Leadership Style:** | 'Rally the troops'<br>Let's all work together |

**Overview of The Loyalist**

Known for their loyalty and commitment, **SIXES** can be very effective team players.

The type **SIX** can be further divided into two personalities. The difference between the two is how they handle fear. The phobic **SIX** will run away from danger, whereas the counter-phobic **SIX** will hesitate, momentarily think about taking action and then tackle it head-on.

They are excellent trouble-shooters and are extremely alert to the kind of things that can go wrong and therefore prepare for them well beforehand. They are very incisive, practical and original thinkers.

However, a constant preoccupation with worst-case scenarios, playing devil's advocate and using mental analysis leads to a detachment from their own inner guidance. This, in turn, leads to procrastination, distrust, paranoia and lack of confidence in their own judgement.

Often a push-pull scenario exists where there is a desire for direction and leadership from others but at the same time a resistance to the same; they like strong leadership but don't like being controlled, and often avoid taking responsibility.

Constantly scanning the environment to maintain a sense of security can produce heightened intuitive awareness of potential dangers, alternative possibilities and new ideas. This could also lead to making unnecessary assumptions that danger and menace lurk in every person, event and circumstance.

When feeling secure within a friendship or team framework they offer loyalty and support for fear of being left alone. At the same time, though, if feeling insecure they often distrust the same people to whom they offer their loyalty.

Healthier personality aspects develop when **SIXES** connect with their inner guidance through working on developing their own inner authority and by accepting insecurity as a natural part of life experience.

**Famous SIXES**

Princess Diana
George W Bush
Woody Allen
Jay Leno
Tom Hanks
Sir John Harvey Jones
Sherlock Holmes
Columbo
Richard Nixon
Sigmund Freud

**Possible Career Preferences**

Police Force
Team sports
Crime Investigator
Technical Support
Analyst

**SIX Organisations**

The CIA
Police Force

## Connected Types

Healthy –**SIXES** take on some of the characteristics of **NINES** (Peacemakers)
Unhealthy – **SIXES** take on some of the characteristics of **EIGHTS** (Achievers)

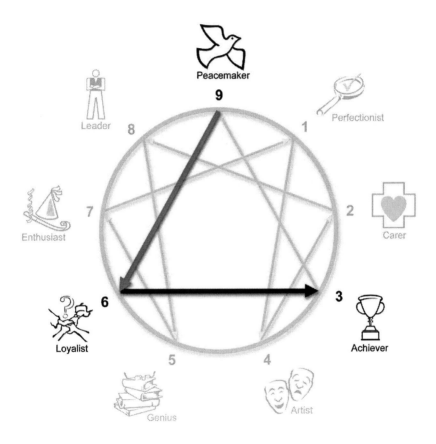

**Healthy**

Strong empathy with others
Can see and acknowledge other people's point of view.
Use genuine humour to access more resourceful emotional states
within people.
Relaxed and grounded with people
Supportive, decisive and valiant in their approach
Self-assured and completely trusting of themselves and the people
they are coaching.

**Average**

Seek reassurance from others
Anxious and needy
Pessimistic about the future and results
Use sarcasm to cover up their fears.
Suspicious of people
Defensive and blame other people for lack of success.
Become involved in power struggles instead of treating the person
they are coaching as equal.

## Unhealthy

Insecure with themselves
Negative and hyper-vigilant
Paranoid that people will not perform well or do what they have
said they will do.
They become workaholics.
Tell lies to cover their own mistakes
Manic in their approach

**The Loyalist Coach**

**Meet David – an IT Team Leader**

David has always been able to solve problems using his strong analytical powers and never have his questioning skills been so valuable than when coaching his team.

Leadership in the past has been difficult, according to David, who prefers to 'muck in' with the team rather than oversee other people. Now, as he understands more about his natural motivational type, he knows how important it is to trust the people around him to do the majority of the daily tasks and be the one who focuses on the team performance.

Playing devil's advocate would get David into trouble with his coaching, because he found that he tended to raise problem issues rather than use his gift to uncover solutions. As a coach and leader he realises that this approach will not move the team forward and keep them motivated.

 He has a knack of being able to appreciate the opposite point of view in any situation or problem and is great at "what if" scenarios. As an IT analyst, focusing on problems rather than solutions had served him well in the past

David is now aware himself when he is over-questioning, and over-analysing and turns his attention to moving things forward.

As he learns to truly trust his own inner sense of authority, David is becoming more open and trusting of the natural flow of events. As a result, the people he is coaching gain confidence in doing their job.

He now understands the difference between wit and sarcasm, vital for **SIXES** who often unintentionally offend people. He now enjoys using his sense of humour to help people feel more relaxed and open to his coaching.

David also has many **SIXES** in his team and is aware of their tendency to blame each other for mistakes or non-performance. Knowing now that this is part of their pattern, David breaks the cycle by engendering full responsibility within individuals through his coaching. An agreement not to blame each other but instead ask the question – "how might I be responsible for this?" is proposed.

A collaborative style of management is now the focus of David's leadership and coaching development. Referring regularly to the healthy traits of a type **NINE** – the peacemaker – he knows that he utilises the best of his skills whenever he decides to trust himself and the people he works with.

**THE LOYALIST**

## PROOF EXERCISES

Make sure you ask the questions that permit the person you are coaching to solve problems for themselves, and trust that they will follow through.

Practice believing in the positive side of situations. As a coach your role is to motivate and you may have a tendency to look for non-existent problems without realising it.

Notice the tendency to blame others if your coaching isn't working. Take responsibility for your coaching style and access more resourceful behaviours by completely opening to the viewpoints of others.

Notice when you are judging people. The moment you judge someone you lose the power to coach effectively.

Learn to trust more in what your gut instincts are telling you, rather than relying too heavily on logical analysis. You will find your coaching is quicker and more effective.

Because a **SIX** likes to feel so much part of the team, he/she often take on too much. If you are not already, become very comfortable with delegating and always leave your coaching interaction with NOTHING to do yourself.

Notice the tendency to ask more questions than are necessary to achieve a result. Keep the coaching brief and trust, trust, trust!

Be patient with others and allow them to move at their pace and not yours.

# THE ENTHUSIAST

> *"I find it impossible to stop my brain from churning through all the ideas and possibilities facing me at any given moment."*
>
> **Richard Branson**

| | |
|---|---|
| **Also known as:** | Eternal Teenager, The Visionary, The Epicure, The Optimist, Adventurer |
| **World View:** | To explore new worlds. The world is an exciting place full of opportunities and new experiences to be had. |
| **Focus on:** | Adventure<br>Seeking pleasurable experiences |
| **Basic Fear:** | Being deprived |
| **Virtues:** | Sobriety |
| **Natural Coaching and Leadership Style:** | Fun loving cheerleaders, motivators, networkers |

## Overview of The Enthusiast

Known for their optimism, playfulness, spontaneity and humour, **SEVENS** have a gift for networking and connecting with people. They are very creative and have a great ability to draw together information from many different sources and synthesise these into new ideas and concepts.

Having an active imagination, they like to keep all options open and have difficulty seeing any downside. They tend to avoid conflict, avoid mundane routine work, hate being criticised, and avoid feelings of pain, not seeing these as opportunities for growth.

They are naturally very fast learners and often have a multitude of projects and activities on the go.

Excessive involvement in so many diverse areas often leads to an inability to decide what is truly important and what to stick with until completion. Although great at the inception of a new project, **SEVENS** find it hard to take it through to completion when, being easily bored, they find another tempting experience or challenge that beckons.

Healthier aspects of the personality develop when they begin to appreciate the now, instead of always planning what to do next, and when they develop the patience and persistence to follow through with projects. Paying more attention to discomfort and negative feelings offers opportunities to see their constant activity as a way of diverting attention from their causes.

## Famous SEVENS
Richard Branson
Anita Roddick
Cliff Richard
Jim Carrey
Robin Williams
Stephen Spielberg
John F Kennedy
Goldie Hawn
Sarah Ferguson
Roger Rabbit

## Possible Career Preferences

Travel Agent
Beautician
Explorer
Fitness Instructor
Public Relations
Acting

## SEVEN Organisations

3M
Ben and Jerry's Ice Cream
Virgin

## Connected Types

Healthy – **SEVENS** take on some of the characteristics of **FIVES** (Genius)
Unhealthy – **SEVENS** take on some of the characteristics of **ONES** (Perfectionists)

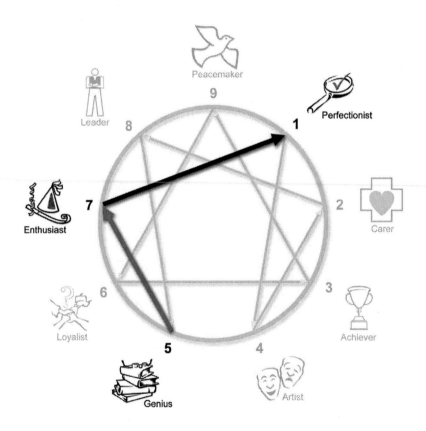

**Healthy**

Appreciative, caring, optimistic and outgoing
Practical
Fun to be with
Big picture planners
Spontaneous and versatile.
Innovative
High energy
Creative


**Average**

Distracted
Opinionated
Showing excitement to cover up feelings of frustration and boredom
Impatient with people and projects
Fidget


**Unhealthy**

Defensive
Self-centred
Frantic in their approach to tasks
Excessive interest in themselves and their physical appearance
Hyper-critical of self and others

**The Enthusiast Coach**
**Meet Sally – Manager of a Fitness Centre**

Sally has worked for her local fitness centre for 2 years. Her genuine enthusiasm and outgoing nature make her an ideal coach.

She approaches coaching creatively and does not hesitate in making the interactions as short and as sweet as possible. Now with her new level of skills she is able to produce results in a matter of moments. When Results Coaching in 60 Seconds is mastered **SEVENS** can experience tremendous variety and achievement without becoming bored.

Sally has a natural ability to synthesise strands of information people provide when coaching and assist people in forming action plans that are realistic and creative at the same time.

Friendly and optimistic, as well as charming, Sally is liked by her team. She has learned to stay enthusiastic by finding a career that truly interests her, something that she can give her full attention to.

Her development is now focused on coaching people in perceived positions of authority, such as clients who hold senior positions in local firms and their line managers. By letting go of fear of confrontation when it arises, she is building confidence.

She is more aware of her tendency to not follow up with her coaching and to avoid this happening makes a point of reviewing her team members on a daily basis.

## THE ENTHUSIAST

## <u>PROOF EXERCISES</u>

Notice the tendency to leave things unfinished. Make sure you have completed each coaching process before moving onto the next and keep your promises to review the person's progress regularly.

Ask others for feedback on your coaching and stay open to their points of view. Even if you do not agree with them, thank them for their feedback and take time to reflect on their comments.

Practice focusing on the here and now. Be grateful for what you have right now.

Be aware of being attracted to coaching people who also have high energy levels. Challenge yourself to openly coach the quieter types.

Set goals for yourself <u>every day</u> and seek support to make sure you follow through.

# *THE LEADER*

*"When placed in command -- take charge."*

**General Norman Schwarzkopf**

| | |
|---|---|
| **Also known as:** | The Boss, The Asserter, The Protector, The Chief |
| **World View:** | I am in charge<br>I defend the weak and expose power abusers<br>The strong survive |
| **Focus on:** | Being self-reliant and being in control |
| **Basic Fear:** | Of being controlled by others. |
| **Virtues:** | Innocence |
| **Natural Coaching and Leadership Style:** | To take charge, bold, to tame the unstable, autocratic, confrontational |

## Overview of the Leader

As the natural leaders, the **EIGHTS** can be truly wonderful visionaries. Known for their charisma, magnetism, magnanimity, independence, leadership and strength, they relish challenges and live with a lust for life and pleasure.

**EIGHTS** often deny any weakness or vulnerability in themselves. They become very assertive, but also very protective of the underdog, or the more vulnerable people in their charge and the qualities they themselves have are the qualities they look for and respect in others.

They prefer others to be open, forceful and direct in their communications. Anger is shown easily, and is over and done with quickly with no grudges being held. They have no problem opposing any authority they disagree with. Rules are for other people to follow.

Excessive focus on controlling others and their environment can lead to unhealthy behaviours such as bullying, manipulation, violence, coercion, breaking the rules to get their own way.

There are some **EIGHTS** who never work for anyone else but themselves. If they do work for someone else, they try to make sure they are at the head of their particular division.

When they feel in control, they are decisive, self-assertive, magnanimous, energising, direct, charismatic, and popular; and they may even display some of their vulnerable side. however, when they feel out of control or under someone else's thumb they can becoming bullying, destructive, manipulative, and engage in a power battle. Compromise is a dirty word and they will stamp their agenda firmly on everyone's mind.

Healthier aspects of the personality evolve as they begin to accept their own vulnerability and express their gentler side, opening up and trusting others more.

| Famous EIGHTS | Possible Career Preferences |
|---|---|
| Martin Luther King | Any leadership role |
| Indira Ghandi | The Armed Forces |
| Anthony Robbins | Political leader |
| Frank Sinatra | Executives |
| Russell Crowe | Sport |
| Charlton Heston | |
| Susan Sarandon | |
| Mike Tyson | **EIGHT Organisation** |
| Arnold Schwarzenegger | |
| Robert Maxwell | Microsoft |
| Boris Yeltsin | Mafia |
| Norman Schwarzkopf | |
| Henry VIII | |
| Adolph Hitler | |
| Saddam Hussain | |

## Connected Types

Healthy – **EIGHTS** take on some of the characteristics of **TWOS** (Carers)
Unhealthy – **EIGHTS** take on some of the characteristics of **FIVES** (Genius)

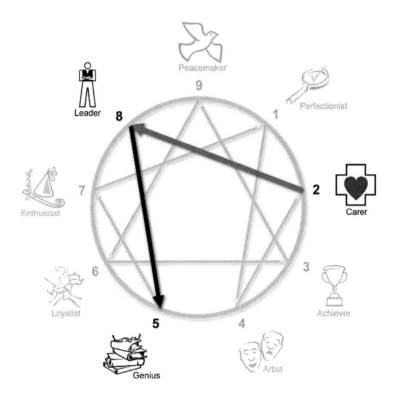

## Healthy

They let go of wanting to control situations and becoming caring about the feelings of others.
Assertive and action-orientated
Strategic and decisive
Protective of the underdog
Constructive and energetic
Loyal, generous and supportive
Forgiving and heroic

## Average

From an **EIGHT's** point of view competitiveness may appear to make them more resourceful, but in fact it can hinder their performance.
Boastful
Demanding and explosive
Pushy and aggressive
Rule breakers
'My way or the highway!'

## Unhealthy

Arrogant
Vengeful towards people
Uncompromising
Fault-finding
Unfeeling and domineering
Bullying

**The Leader Coach**

**Meet Sam : Senior Executive of a High Tech Company in London**

Sam is now a remarkable coach and has developed his skills by using true compassion to guide and encourage performance through his senior team.

Sam still has a strong desire to control the people around him and likes to know where he stands with everyone. He hates being deceived. Sam would lead his team by taking charge at every opportunity. Coaching has raised his awareness of the need to allow others to take that responsibility.

**EIGHTS** have a black-or-white attitude to what is fair and not fair, leaving little room for any middle ground. In the past, this would cause a breakdown in communication, with Sam refusing to allow for the other people's point of view. In coaching, their point of view must always be taken into account.

Strength, vision, leadership and a sense of justice are Sam's greatest assets. When he balances these traits with patience and more kindness towards his colleagues, his team responds well.

**EIGHTS** explode without thinking of the consequences of their actions. This makes people afraid to say what they believe is right, for fear of being 'shot down'. This still happens to Sam, but less often as he learns to control his anger, when he feels impatience or frustration rising up.

A great benefit to Sam has been sharing Enneagram profiles with his team members, so they understand his leadership style better and can work to complement that style rather than being fearful of it. We rarely find two **EIGHTS** in any team and so their behaviour can seem radically different to others. His team is learning to be more direct and stand up for itself. This helps diffuses a situation, remembering the **EIGHT's** preference for bluntness. An **EIGHT** has no time for beating around the bush or someone not saying what they mean.

Sam still knows that his strong desire to control people may well reduce others' confidence, instead of building it up. When he takes a more gentle and empathetic approach he now realises that he has just as much chance if not more that the results that he and the coachee really wants will be achieved without experiencing any anger or frustration.

**THE LEADER**

**PROOF EXERCISES**

Note when you are acting on impulse and when you have a tendency to react impulsively, without thinking first. When coaching take just a few seconds to think things through a little before asking questions.

Beware of the tendency to make unrealistic demands on people. Pay attention to any frustration or anger that arises and use the emotion to appropriately let go of the need to control the other person's experience.

Pay attention and notice when people become uncomfortable. Be open with them about your own vulnerabilities and notice how they respond better to you when you acknowledge that.

When coaching, motivate people consistently by showing your appreciation of them and congratulating them regularly on what they have achieved, even if it has not been to the standard you expected.

Become outstanding at validating other people's views and experiences and use them to build their confidence in themselves.

Avoid blaming others. Take full responsibility for the impact your coaching style has on the performance of others. Show more of your compassion and notice how people respond to you.

# THE PEACEMAKER

> *"I claim not to have controlled events, but confess plainly that events have controlled me."*
>
> **Abraham Lincoln**

| | |
|---|---|
| **Also known as:** | The Mediator, The Negotiator, The Empathizer |
| **World View:** | If everyone stays calm and connected and it will all work out |
| **Focus on:** | Keeping the 'peace'<br>Merging with others |
| **Basic Fear:** | Not belonging |
| **Virtues:** | Caring |
| **Natural Coaching and Leadership Style:** | Participatory, reactive, sometimes passive-aggressive |

## Overview of the Peacemaker

Potentially the most elegant in their approach to life are the **NINES**. They have an extraordinary ability to understand the other point of view - so well that when they truly focus themselves and others clearly, they produce quite remarkable results.

**NINES** are known for their tremendous patience, ability to be non-judgemental, and to embrace a wide variety of not only different opinions but also paradoxes. They rarely get sidetracked by extremes, thus making excellent peacemakers and negotiators.

Of all the types, the **NINES** find it easiest to empathise with all the others and can enter each of their worldview very easily. They know how to support and get the best out of people working with them. The **NINES** are easygoing and their accepting nature makes others feel at ease with them.

The desire to get along with others can lead to an inability to take a position on an issue. There is a fear of saying no and producing an angry reaction, which leads to a suppression or denial of any personal agenda or desire.

There is a tendency to minimise the importance of personal goals when others' request and demands seem more urgent. Anger is shown indirectly through passive aggression rather than direct confrontation.

Seeing both the positive and negatives equally well, on all sides of an issue, can lead to procrastination and indecisiveness and sometimes being diverted into trivial unimportant activity, at the cost of progress towards a goal.

## Famous NINES

Bill Clinton
Ronald Reagan
Sir Winston Churchill
Queen Elizabeth II
Prince Charles
Abraham Lincoln
Kofi Annan
John Major
Alfred Hitchcock
Kevin Costner
Gerald Ford
John Goodman
Homer Simpson

## Possible Career Preferences

Of all the types, **NINES** are the ones who relate to ALL of the other types and as such we find **NINES** in a wide variety of different roles.
HR Managers
Negotiators

## NINE Organisation

Postal Service

**Connected Types**

Healthy – **NINES** take on some of the characteristics of **THREES** (Achievers)
Unhealthy – **NINES** take on some of the characteristics of **SIXES** (Loyalists)

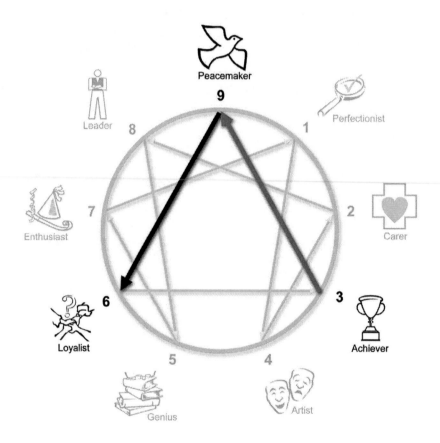

## Healthy

Highly empathetic and humble
Unaffected by the emotional responses of others
Focused and productive
Self-confident
Dynamic and positive
Level-headed with people
Very calm and patient

## Average

Fear of conflict
Afraid to hold somebody else to a commitment
Afraid to push somebody in one-to-one interactions
Indecisive
Downplaying of problems to avoid conflict

## Unhealthy

Passive aggressive
Emotionally numb
Stubborn
Lazy/apathetic
Unaware of own basic needs

**The Peacemaker Coach**
**Meet Simon – Vice President of a Manufacturing Company**

Simon has a desire for everyone to get along well with each other and as such he adopts a highly cooperative coaching style. His gift is a natural ability to relate to everyone in his team.

Simon's continual focus on appeasing others and being able to understand and reflect concerns leads to a pronounced ability to empathise fully with many views; however, this makes it difficult to take a personal position on any issue. This leads to compromise, procrastination and slow decision making, it being easier to decide what is not wanted rather than what is. He realises his need to become more assertive in his coaching

To avoid conflict, Simon has often allowed people (including himself) off the hook at critical moments. This tactic has had a long-term effect on the behaviour of his team, who know what they can get away with.

**NINES** prefer to prioritise things as they go. In meetings this can lead to team members feeling confused and lacking the clarity of direction they need to work effectively as a team.

He addresses both of these areas by focusing his behaviour on the positive aspects of the **THREE** profile (that of the Achiever, the point the **NINE** moves towards when operating from the healthy aspect of their profile) taking a more effective, direct, focused and goal-orientated approach.

With this mindset, Simon gets less carried away with other people's agenda and pays attention to his own needs and those of the business. He is amazed at the resulting reduction in conflict.

## THE PEACEMAKER

## PROOF EXERCISES

Notice your tendency to be over-accommodating towards people, to avoid conflict. Remember the people you are coaching may present many smoke screens as reasons for not achieving objectives, and you must be willing to challenge people for their own good.

Ask yourself on a daily basis, what am I going to complete by the end of today? Review your progress throughout and at the end of each day. This will begin to instil the importance of follow-through within yourself, so that you can then reinforce this skill with others.

When coaching ensure that you are sticking to the priorities of the person you are coaching and any related business objectives. **NINES** have a tendency to be easily sidetracked and must remain focused throughout the interaction. A good tip is to write down the objective and keep referring to it.

**NINES** are wonderful at responding to the requests of others. Be proactive and take responsibility for changing situations instead of hoping things will change by themselves.

Learn the value of saying what you want and practice saying 'no' to people. People will feel comfortable with you for this and it may have the effect of drawing them towards you even more. Value your own time for recharging your energy, to be able to give the best of yourself consistently.

To support you in focusing consistently on your agenda seek coaching for yourself.

When goal setting pay attention to times when you are focusing on what you do not want, as opposed to what you do want. Write everything down to form a clear picture of what you are aiming for.

# Chapter Five

Relate
. Managing your Coaching Relationships

Remember you are in <u>partnership</u> with the people in your team that you serve.

The first of the eights steps within the Results Coaching in 60 Seconds model is Relate. This is about having complete rapport with the person you are coaching so that trust and openness can exist and be maintained throughout the entire coaching process.

Without rapport your coachee will close down to your questions and show signs of resistance to being coached. The degree to which you can establish rapport quickly is one in which you can effectively complete the coaching process successfully in under a minute.

In order to consistently produce results in less than 60 seconds, one of your primary objectives is to create supportive environments around you. If your relationships with the individuals are strong enough, this step will happen with little effort on your part.

If there are some people in your team or you have particular coaching clients you find it hard to relate to and understand, then mastery of this step will give you the skills and knowledge to connect quickly with everyone in your team and open them to your coaching.

This step will also increase your ability to empathise in such a way that your coachee clearly perceives you understand how they feel and accept their point of view. You may not agree with their point of view but you can remain objective and open, giving you fuller access to your intuition and personal resources to coach them effectively.

## How we make sense of the World

Richard Bandler and John Grinder, the founders of what is now known as NeuroLinguistic Programming (NLP), were both interested in psychotherapy. Their research into the successful working practices of leading therapists led them to discover powerful tools for understanding how the mind works. They found that people perceive the world around them in three ways; visually, auditorily, and kinaesthetically; that is, through sight, sounds and feelings.

These 'modalities' are the means by which we organise the information that we receive. Although we use all three modalities, we tend to prefer one over the others. This is not a conscious choice we make. As a coach, if you know which of these is your coachee's preferred modality, you have a very powerful edge in being able to communicate in the way they subconsciously respond best to.

## Aligning our Language to that of the Coachee

When we communicate we use words that create pictures (VISUAL), describe sounds (AUDITORY), or give a sense of what we feel (KINAESTHETIC).

Paying attention to what words people are using and aligning your language patterns to match theirs increases the level of rapport you have with them. This is called 'Matching'. Miscommunication happens when two people talking about the same subject are mismatching each other in the way they describe their point of view ,even though their viewpoints may actually be the same.

E.g.
**Mismatching:**

Sam (Coachee):     "I feel <u>uncomfortable</u> with using slides. I am really not <u>confident</u> presenting in front of people."

John (Coach):                "What if we take a closer <u>look</u> at your presentation and you can practice <u>showing</u> me how you would use the slides?"

John's intention is good but his visual mode of communication is not in line with Sam's kinaesthetic mode. Consequently, she will not be as open to his coaching.

**Matching:**

Sam (Coachee):    "I feel <u>uncomfortable</u> with using slides. I am really not <u>confident</u> with presenting in front of people."
John (Coach):              "I understand why you may feel uncomfortable. What needs to happen to give you more confidence and allow you to feel more comfortable with this?

Now Sam will feel as though she has been more understood.

## PROOF EXERCISE – Level One

Pay attention to people around you and observe their language patterns. Identify whether they are speaking more about what they see, hear or feel and note down a few words you would use to relate more effectively with them.

The following table gives you some suggestions.

| VISUAL (Anything that describes what a person can see) "I see what you mean" | AUDITORY (Anything that describes what a person can hear) "I hear what you are saying" | KINAESTHETIC (Anything that describes what a person can feel) "I know how you feel" |
|---|---|---|
| Colours (Red, blue etc). | Hear | Feel |
| Large Small | Sound | Sense |
| Bright Dark | Loud | Knowing |
| Show | Ringing | Confident |
| See | Tell | Scared |
| Curved/Round (Shapes) | Talk | Nervous |
| Light/Shade | Conversation | Happy/Unhappy |
| Clear/Foggy | Saying | Rough/Smooth |
| Patterned/Plain | Tone | Tired |

Similarly you can find sensory-based phrases that fit into the above categories.

## VISUAL

I see what you mean.
We see eye-to-eye here.
It's quite clear to me.
You paint a very bright picture of the situation!
Let's take a look at the big picture.
I can see no end to this.
The future is bright.
That's a sight for sore eyes.
No shadow of doubt.
It came to me in a flash.
It's a blind spot with him.

## AUDITORY

That rings a bell.
Music to my ears.
I hear you.
Tell me what you mean.
Tell me word for word.
Express yourself clearly.
Loud and clear.
It's all Greek to me.
He's on a different wavelength.
Let me sound him out on this.

## KINAESTHETIC

I can't get a handle on this.
I feel for him.
I get a sense of what he's after.
I get a gut feeling about this.
Do you get a sense of this?
He's thick-skinned.
It was a heated argument.
She's a cool customer.
Control yourself.
Do you follow me?
Time to make a move.

It is quite simple to know if someone is thinking in pictures, sounds or feelings.

When visualising things from the past we tend to move our eyes up and to our left.

When imagining a future event or making up a picture, we move our eyes upwards and to our right.

Someone staring straight ahead but not focused on anything also indicates visualisation.

Similarly, when remembering sounds from the past, our eyes move across to our left.

When imagining how something would sound we look to our right.

Our eyes go down to our right when we are accessing feelings.

When talking to ourselves our eyes move down to our left.

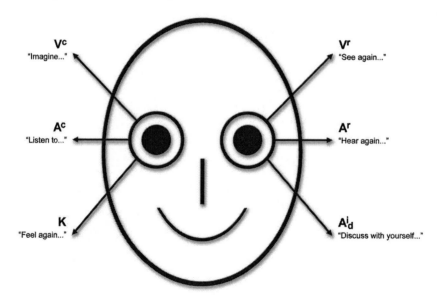

When asking questions of someone, note the eye movements before you have finished asking the question, as these movements tend to occur very quickly.

A good way to practice is to watch television interviews closely. Note the kinds of words used by the interviewer and the eye movements of the interviewee in response to the questions.

## PROOF EXERCISE – Level Two

Having practiced matching the language patterns, now turn your attention to the vocal volume, tone and pace of people you are talking with.

Whether they speak fast or slow, loud or soft matches their communication style and you will considerably increase the chances of developing very quick rapport.

## Aligning Your Coaching Questions

Rapport can be further increased by being creative and aligning your coaching questions. Your coachee can understand and relate more quickly to the questions you ask.

E.g.

| Coachee's statement | Ideal Response |
|---|---|
| "I feel like all doors are closing around me." | "What needs to happen to keep these doors open?" |
| "I can't see the wood for the trees?" | "Yes, and now it's time to cut back some of the trees so you can see clearly and move forward." |
| " I am drowning in a sea of paper." | "Let me throw you a life jacket and help you to pull yourself out!" |

Now, reflect on a time when a person has said 'no' to you. How did it make you feel in that moment? It probably triggered an emotional state within you. You did not feel good and maybe for even a moment or two made it impossible for you to respond.

'Yes' and 'No' are two of the most common words in the English language. One of them builds self-esteem the other can destroy it, if not immediately, then over time.

Great coaches understand the often fragile nature and importance of others' self-esteem and for this reason you would be well advised to never use the word 'No'.

How much more effective your coaching would be if you could use language patterns that keep your coachee open and positive at all times? This can be as easy as dropping the word 'no' from your vocabulary and using alternatives such as 'yes', and ' what about…..?' A person's experience is always right from their point of view so you can feel comfortable in agreeing with whatever they say and then replace 'no' with "yes, and" followed by another question. Hypnotists use language patterns with clients such as 'that's right.' in order to keep open the subconscious mind and prevent defensiveness arising in the other.

Your language patterns will impact on how your coachee feels. What you are aiming for is that, over time, the vast majority of interactions with you are fun and pleasurable. They then associate only good things happening to them when they see or call you.

Using positive words such as confidence, yes, relaxed, happy and so on will bring into play these feelings in yourself and the people around you. We will explore further other language patterns and strategies that help you do this.

**PROOF EXERCISE**

Observe people communicating and notice the way they describe things to each other. Make a note of them and create 'ideal' response questions, in the context of what they said, which would be useful to ask if you were coaching them.

All it takes is practice to notice the context, rather then getting emotionally involved in the content of what they are saying. Listen to the words they use and you will find yourself with less emotional attachment to the situation, letting you maintain more of your natural coaching state and communicate with them effectively.

## Knowing how People are feeling

It is easy to assume we know how someone else is feeling, but without imagining what it would feel like to be in his or her shoes we can only make a guess. Only guessing what people are feeling makes coaching a hit-or-miss process.

Imagine being in the body of a cat walking around a beautiful garden. Notice how low you are to the ground and what you can see from this perspective that you wouldn't see as a human being. Notice how the smell of the grass is stronger and sweeter at this level and how the grass feels under your paws. Now feel what it feels like to hear a dog barking behind you!

Just as we can match a person's language patterns, so we can match their movements, posture and breathing to give an accurate reading of how they are feeling and create even more rapport between the two of you.

We have all experienced times when we thought a person was committed to something and then found afterwards that they had broken the agreement. What if you could spot those signs the moment agreements are first made? And increase your chances of having them keep their agreements and produce results every time?

It is about making sure that their body language is always giving you the same messages as the words they are saying and the tonality with which they say them.

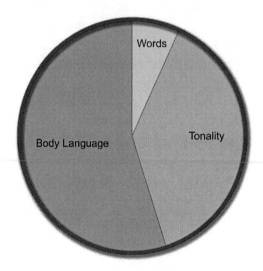

7% of the meaning of our communication is carried in the words we use, 38% in the tonality in which we say those words and 55% in our physiology (body language). We know a person is telling the truth when their body language is perfectly aligned with what they say and how they say it.

Developing your sensory acuity increases your awareness when coaching, so you can spot subtle signals that tell you a person is not 100% congruent in what they are saying to you. Without their completed congruency you reduce the chances of producing results.

Have you noticed that when you are relaxed and enjoying the good company of a friend that both your bodies have assumed the same posture? In fact, the deeper the rapport, the greater the similarities between both you and the coachee.

A great coach will naturally create this kind of trust-building rapport, by matching their coachee. This is not the same as mimicry, which is an exaggerated copying of movements. Matching is subtly adopting similar attributes such as head, neck, hand, arm, leg positions, weight distribution, breathing rate, voice qualities and so on.

## PROOF EXERCISE

Observe people in a relaxed environment having fun. This may be in a bar or restaurant over the weekend. Identify people in complete rapport with each other and notice how they are copying each other's body movement without realising it. Your aim is to create this level of rapport with each and every coachee.

*Having this level of rapport will allow you to:*

- Know how the person is feeling throughout the entire interaction
- Know to what level they are motivated and committed to achieving results
- Know when you need to ask more questions to further increase that level of motivation and commitment to achieve the results
- Have more natural confidence and ability to increase their level of motivation
- You remain open with them and they remain open to you
- Both enjoy coaching!

**Developing successful Coaching Relationships**

The level of rapport you have with your coachees is a reflection of how well you relate to and understand their 'model of the world' i.e. their way of seeing things. As a coach and team leader it is your responsibility to understand them and their communication strategies.

*'Seek first to understand, then to be understood'*

*- Stephen Covey*

Identifying which relationships require more of your attention gives you the opportunity to focus on understanding their model of the world and have rapport with them immediately, so you can make better use of Results Coaching in 60 Seconds techniques.

Reviewing the quality of your coaching relationships as a business manager, on a regular basis, gives you a clear picture of three important aspects: how fair you are as a leader, how committed you are to your team and their level of commitment both to you and the business results.

This simple tool provides you with an overview of exactly where you are right now with each and every relationship. Getting a sense of how balanced or unbalanced, strong or weak your coaching relationships are then takes no more than a few minutes.

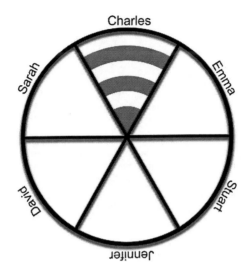

Draw a circle and divide it into segments. Each segment relates to individual team members. The further you draw a line towards the outside edge of this circle, the stronger your perceived relationship with that individual. Complete all segments and you have a picture of how balanced and strong your coaching relationships are.

This example shows a coach/manager having an uncomfortable ride on a daily basis!

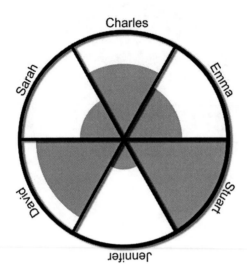

The Seven Habits of Highly Effective People is Stephen Covey's best-known and most popular book. If you have not yet read it then I highly recommend that you take a look.

One of his many unique concepts, the emotional bank account, is a metaphor for the amount of trust that has been built up and the feeling of safety in a relationship. When trust is high it makes communication easier, instant and effective.

It highlights the importance of making regular deposits in individual and team accounts, thereby increasing the credit balance on a daily basis. A deposit can be made by showing courtesy and kindness as well demonstrating qualities such as honesty and keeping commitments. A withdrawal, however, is made by showing disrespect, betraying trust, discourtesy or threatening behaviour.

What are you doing to increase Emotional Bank Account deposits, to increase rapport and strengthen your working relationships with people on a daily basis?

Coaching relationships require small amounts of success to be stacked so that your coachee's confidence in you grows over time. You may want to work with them on smaller objectives and build up the value of your success together. The cumulative effect of your results will be considerably higher.

## The Art of Breaking Rapport

*"How do you demonstrate respect? Through the integrity of the message you communicate. It sounds simplistic, but we have found the easiest way of getting things done was by being straight."*

*Bob Galvin, Motorola*

If you have made enough deposits in a person's Emotional Bank Account then making a withdrawal occasionally will not hurt. In fact there are times when it may benefit both you and the coachee to make a perceived withdrawal, to achieve a result through coaching.

We all love talking about ourselves. As a coach, breaking rapport is about knowing when someone's long story about a past event is hindering their own ability to access the best of themselves and consequently handle their current situation. Ultimately, they are merely reasons why they believe they cannot do something.

Many people will tell you their story, but by listening to negative stories you are reinforcing their behaviour and limiting them. This can also be the reason your coaching is taking far too long.

When a person tells a story about their past, the emotions associated with that event surface. If this event did not serve them at the time, then the same emotional state will not help find clear answers to improve the situation right now. Remember, you cannot solve a problem with the same mindset that created it! Their story is effectively a trance and if you go into this trance with them then you stand less chance of pulling them out of it!

Occasionally you may decide to break rapport with a person, just to get them out of their trance. The stronger your overall relationship with a person, the more outrageous you can be with them when breaking their habitual patterns of behaviour.

Using elegant pattern-interrupts, such as making them laugh to distract their attention, will change their focus 'in that moment'. If you interrupt the pattern enough times, you will change their conditioning long-term so effectively that they will never have the same negative feelings about that past event again.

I once had a team where two out of the group of ten were so negative about the day that it was impacting on the rest of the group. I suggested they take a break and a walk to decide how committed they were to the programme. If they felt they were not 100% committed, then they should also consider the impact of their attitude on the entire group. I then gave them the option of attending the day or not.

If these words appear too strong, then consider the positive tonality with which they were said and also my body language, which indicated that I had their best interests at heart. Remember, it is not the words you say, it is the way you say it, combined with the message conveyed by your body language. This combination is what people register and read your intention from and my highest intention was for the good of everyone in that room – including myself.

As a result of this form of pattern-interrupt, the two in question returned to the room more open and in a far more resourceful frame of mind.

These techniques should be used as a last resort, but do not be afraid to use them if you are finding it difficult to open people up to your coaching.

Be creative, explore various ways to change your coachee's focus. By developing this method you can quickly change their emotional state from one of fear or discomfort to at the least neutrality, enabling you to open the doors of possibility in their mind. Help them to learn from the past, focus on the present moment and coach them into designing a compelling future.

**Summary for Relate**

**Three important things to remember:**

1.  Match and mirror coachee body and language patterns to create instant rapport and develop more of your own intuition.

2.  Take full responsibility for the quality of your coaching relationships, review them regularly and continue to strengthen them every day.

3.  Create confidence and have your coachee maintain complete faith in you as a coach by keeping your commitments, being honest and focusing on guaranteed results that build momentum over time.

# Chapter Six

# Relating to each of the Enneagram Types

> "Whether or not we realize it each of us has a special gift inside us just waiting to surface!...We owe developing these gifts not only to ourselves, but those around us as well... The important thing here is not what your gift is as much as that you develop it so that you can share it with those around you and in the process further your own personal life! Once we have identified our special talents it doesn't matter whether or not we find immediate success in them, what does matter is that we take a step each day towards our intended goal!"
>
> **- Josh Hinds**

The Enneagram gives us further clues as to how we can relate more to people based on their type. However, before you can use it effectively with your coaching you must identify the Enneagram types of the people in your team.

### How to recognise each Enneagram Type

The following pointers are generalisations of what to look for in each type.

When people are showing more of the very healthy aspects of their type, it is not that easy to immediately tell the difference between them. Therefore, as you read the comments below, bear in mind that the 'negative' descriptions are describing behaviour and appearance as influenced by the Enneagram pattern, and in particular where the individual is at the average or unhealthy level of awareness.

## THE PERFECTIONIST

Crisp and clean appearance
Straight and erect bearing
Thin-lipped. Often purse their lips to hold back anger
Polite and well-mannered
Often sit with legs together or crossed
Can have a sermonising or preaching speaking style
May point their finger when talking
Critical of themselves and others
Self-righteous

## THE CARER

Socially extrovert and outwardly friendly
Often the first to approach you and offer you refreshment at a gathering
First to offer to pay for things
Proactive in helping others
Choose gifts very carefully
May give to people with the motive of receiving something in return
Show pride in being indispensable to others

Put others before themselves
Seductive
Adjust themselves to the expectations of others

 **THE ACHIEVER**

They often wear designer clothes and expensive jewellery
Extrovert
Status-driven
Boastful of their achievements
Work at high speed
Workaholics
Competitive

 **THE ARTIST**

Dress extrovertly and flamboyantly so that they look different from others
Elegant and classy
In their effort to be different they may go to extremes
Often interested in the arts, music and drama
Associate themselves with experts and connoisseurs
Envious of others
The most outwardly emotional of all the types
Attracted to the sad side of life

**THE GENIUS**

Often perceived as 'nerd-like' and 'geekish' in their appearance
Have extreme detailed knowledge of their field of work or leisure.
Introvert
Private
Often thin and wiry appearance, pale complexion
Make do with the bare essentials in every day life
Find it very difficult to get in touch with their emotions
Appear detached emotionally
Prefer to observe rather than actively engage themselves.

 **THE LOYALIST**

Frequently scan the room unconsciously looking for signs of danger
Avoid eye contact
Worried
Sarcastic when they feel threatened, witty and funny when they are relaxed
Play devil's advocate and run worst-case scenarios
Find it hard to trust people
Find it hard to take responsibility
Cynical attitude to what may be new or different

**THE ENTHUSIAST**

Often look much younger than they are
Fun loving and outgoing
Life and soul of the party
Short attention span – easily distracted
Rapid talkers
Find it hard to finish things
Manic
Can have a hardwired smile
Get bored easily
Seek variety every day

 **THE LEADER**

Assertive/aggressive
Sometimes a strong, stocky, dominating physique
Controlling
Assume a leadership role
Impulsive and brash
Easily show anger
Most often found in senior positions within a team
Protective of the underdog and those they perceive as vulnerable
Compassionate and caring when open to others

**THE PEACEMAKER**

Laid-back
Passive aggressive – they may say 'yes' when they actually mean 'no'
May agree to something and go off and do their own thing anyway
Rarely get angry
Lazy to their own agenda
Do anything to avoid conflict
Gentle, calm, simple
Can be very quiet in meetings unless asked for their view


## PROOF EXERCISE

Make a list of the people in your team or that you coach regularly, and then take an educated guess as to their Enneagram type. This greater awareness will help you to communicate better with them and therefore improve the effectiveness of your coaching.

It is important, however, to recognize the limitations of this knowledge, it is not advisable to put people into a box and assume that this observed behaviour permanently defines who they are. Stay open to the fact that people are much more than these patterns, which in themselves serve as useful guidelines.

Let people in your team know about the Enneagram and ask them to complete the questionnaire in this book. Then ask them to tell you the two type descriptions they relate to the most. Compare their conclusions to your own and discuss your findings.

The Enneagram is a tool for self-discovery and as such we recommend that you never tell a person what you believe their Enneagram type to be but allow them to discover it for themselves.


## Preferred 'Relate' Styles for each of the Enneagram Types

As this will be a new concept which needs getting used to, we have put together case studies for each Enneagram type to assist you in developing an 'Enneagram coaching perspective'.

The detailed knowledge of how your team or coachees prefer to communicate and be coached will help you to build a quick rapport which can be maintained throughout the coaching process.

Whilst these are business examples, exactly the same principles can be applied to life coaching or even family coaching!

We recommend that you use the matching and mirroring skills mentioned in the previous chapter, together with the basic NLP principles, in conjunction with the Enneagram profiles. Practice using these tools in combination and you will be able to develop masterful communication skills you can use across all areas of business and which will prove invaluable in your life.

# THE PERFECTIONIST

- Be honest with them at all times
- Use a structured approach to your coaching
- Acknowledge the fact they have high expectations
- Praise them for their ability to do what is 'right'
- Allow them to express their anger
- Show appreciation using formal language such as 'you have met all criteria.'
- Talk about projects
- Use plenty of detail
- Assure them they are doing the right things
- Always be punctual
- Emphasise practical solutions
- Consider straightforward approaches
- Keep your commitments
- Be playful in your approach

## WARNING

Never:
- Criticise them
- Question their integrity.
- Display unprincipled behaviour

## Suggested words to use with a type ONE person.

| | | | | |
|---|---|---|---|---|
| Excellence | Light hearted | Right | Process | Organised |
| Ideal | Fun | Rules | Planning | What if? |
| Structure | Agree | Commitment | Projects | Straightforward |

## THE CARER

- Be warm and friendly
- Let them know you care
- Give them regular feedback
- Commend them for their service to others
- Thank them regularly
- Praise them for giving advice and guidance
- Use a face-to-face approach whenever you can
- Acknowledge their talents
- Spend time getting to know them
- Offer to do something nice for them
- Use laughter to help relax them

**WARNING**

Never:
- Use excessive flattery
- Take them for granted
- Make idle, impersonal chit-chat
- Forget to say thank you

**Suggested words to use with a type TWO person**

| | | | | |
|---|---|---|---|---|
| People | Gifts | Well done | Adaptable | Genuine |
| Caring | Favours | Great | Feelings | Confident |
| Love | Enthusiasm | Flexible | Motivated | |

# THE ACHIEVER

- Be outgoing and sociable
- Be quick and direct with your coaching
- Catch them in between tasks and not in the middle of something
- Praise their confidence, energy and enthusiasm regularly.
- Avoid getting into competition with them
- Be positive
- Use time efficiently
- Let them decide how things should be done
- Compliment their ability to handle pressure
- Be assertive with your communication at all times
- Socialise with them whenever possible
- Talk about the opportunities

## WARNING

- Avoid expressing anger with them.
- Note that they consider their achievements to be of more value than their relationships.
- Avoid talking negatively with them.
- Never ignore them
- Never focus on their failures
- Never suggest that they are a loser

## Suggested words to use with a type THREE person

| | | | | |
|---|---|---|---|---|
| Best | Status | Achieve | Success | Strategy |
| Number One | Competition | Do it! | Goals | Win |
| Challenge | Focus | Ultimate | Outstanding | Amazing |

# THE ARTIST

- Make friends with them by taking time to understand them
- Be positive and make every interaction a positive experience
- Allow them to talk about the past
- Invite them to express their feelings and show that you are comfortable with that
- Consult with them
- Acknowledge their special talents
- Be personal in your approach
- Make your approach with them different to others as best you can.
- Use recognition strategies often
- Acknowledge their ability to be able to handle intense emotions
- Allow them freedom for self-expression
- Take a little more time generally with them
- Remember they prefer one-to-one attention
- Accept their ideas without judgement
- Make them feel different and special
- Be gentle
- Compliment them on their creative successes

## WARNING

- Recognise their tendencies to withdraw into themselves and allow them to do so.
- Never try to show yourself to be better than them
- Never be rude or insensitive

- Their self-worth is often tied in with the product of their creative self-expression, and they can be very sensitive to criticism of their work.

## Suggested words to use with a type FOUR person

| Special | Creative | Self Expression | Individual | Compassion |
|---------|----------|-----------------|------------|------------|
| Unique | Intuition | Artistic | Empathy | Refined |
| Different | Beautiful | Appreciate | Recognition | Introspective |

## THE GENIUS

- Always coach a **FIVE** in private and never in an open area in view of others.
- Do not expect emotional language or responses from **FIVES.**
- Be direct with them and very precise.
- Avoid lengthy warm-ups – just get straight to it!
- It is good to let them know beforehand you wish to coach them.
- Share reflections and ideas
- Make observations
- Take time to listen to them
- Take an intelligent approach
- Give them time to answer your questions
- Talk about plans and projects
- Explore theories
- Use logic and facts as opposed to feelings
- Discuss genuinely similar interests.
- Use facts to present your point


## WARNING

Never:
- Question their knowledge or competence. Their biggest fear is that someone else knows more about their specialist subject or area of interest than they do. Acknowledge their expertise.
- Intrude into their space
- Organise things for them

## Suggested words to use with a type FIVE person

| | | | | |
|---|---|---|---|---|
| Intelligent | Genius | Analyse | Objective | Process |
| Think | Thoughtful | Sensitive | Wise | Persevere |
| Logic | Expert | Perceptive | Private | Precise |

## THE LOYALIST

- Self-disclosure will open up a relationship between you and a type **SIX** person because they begin to trust you more.
- Be open and honest with them at all times.
- Emphasise loyalty and trust
- Do what you can to make them feel safe and secure on a daily basis
- Recognise their punctuality
- Gain their collaboration
- Allow them to rely on other's authority when making decisions
- Be friendly
- Use humour
- Be willing to defend and protect them
- Be reliable and show genuine concern for them when appropriate
- You must be totally congruent with everything you say to a **SIX** because they may be constantly on the lookout for danger, hidden agendas and ulterior motives.
- Keep all your agreements because if you lose their trust you may find it very difficult to regain it.
- Should they break the rules then calmly go over the agreement you made, without judgement.
- Make it easy for them to make decisions.
- Stay grounded

**WARNING**

- Avoid mixed messages – always be very clear with your communication
- Never put undue pressure on them
- Never be evasive

**Suggested words to use with a type SIX person**

| Trust | Open | Helpful | Caring | Focus |
| Team | Honest | Responsible | Clear | Support |
| Loyal | Logical | Warm | Direction | Commitment |

# THE ENTHUSIAST

- Have fun with them.
- Coach and think fast with a **SEVEN**
- Share some of your experiences with them. They appreciate self-disclosure. It allows them to feel they are more involved in the process.
- Be outgoing
- Use positive language
- Be enthusiastic
- Talk about the bigger pictures
- Keep excited about the future
- Discuss alternatives
- Look on the bright side of things when times are a little difficult
- Be lively

## WARNING

- Avoid criticism and talking about routine work
- Never ignore them
- Never restrict their freedom or limit their choices
- Never be pessimistic

## Suggested words to use with a type SEVEN person

| Fun | Lively | New | Energetic | Generous |
|-----|--------|-----|-----------|----------|
| Enthusiasm | Adventure | Experience | Support | Exciting |
| Curious | Variety | Spontaneous | Productive | Freedom |
| | | Action-packed | | |

## THE LEADER

- Always keep your promises and appointments with them
- Match their energy and intensity in face-to-face interactions. You will get the respect you deserve
- Be clear and direct
- Admire them and show them respect
- Always admit if you make a mistake and then move on
- Leave them alone when they want to be alone
- Be outgoing and sociable
- Be assertive with every interaction
- Be fair
- Enjoy challenging them
- Give them adequate knowledge to make their decisions
- Praise their courage and strength
- Allow them to present their views
- Allow them to feel in charge

## WARNING

Never:
- Tell them what they cannot do
- Take advantage of them
- Try to con them
- Be indecisive with them
- Act like a wimp

## Suggested words to use with a type EIGHT person

| Straight | Leadership | Protect | Support | Drive |
| Vision | Control | Action | Master | Courage |
| Challenge | Strong | Focus | Loyal | Independent |

## THE PEACEMAKER

- Take your time and be gentle with them
- Speak slowly
- **NINES** have a tendency to meander and go off-track. Allow them to do so and find ways to elegantly bring them back on track as soon as possible
- Be honest and genuine
- Always give them your undivided attention.
- Ask for feedback as it is rarely given voluntarily (for fear of creating conflict)
- Use negotiation often
- Be calm and relaxed at all times
- Settle disagreements as soon as possible
- Use agreeable and familiar topics
- Allow them to talk about themselves
- Emphasise similarities where possible
- Acknowledge their needs and interests
- Listen to their views and opinions

## WARNING

- **NINES** will do anything to avoid confrontation so do whatever you can to avoid loosing your temper with them
- Never put pressure on them
- Never make them feel pushed aside

## Suggested words to use with a type NINE person

| | | | | |
|---|---|---|---|---|
| Peaceful | Agreement | Patience | Control | Empathy |
| Pleasant | Calm | Open-minded | Accept | Support |
| Diplomatic | Relaxed | Negotiate | Wise | Non-judgement |

# Chapter Seven

## Stipulate
### Creating a razor-sharp Focus within yourself and others

> *"The indispensable first step to getting the things you want out of this life is this: decide what you want."*
>
> **Ben Stein**

If there is one aspect of coaching that trips people up more than any other it is not clarifying a powerful vision with the coachee that builds confidence and catalyses action.

Here are some questions you should be asking yourself as a coach:

How outcome-driven are you?
How often do you begin your day knowing exactly what you want to finish today?
What are your goals for business and your personal life?
Before going into meetings have you considered specific outcomes or do you have a list of things to talk about that are more focused on activity?

Think of yourself in terms of an airline pilot, who sets off on his journey with a plane full of passengers, knowing exactly where he is going and throughout the entire flight refers to markers en route that let him know he is on the right track.

Do the people you are coaching and leading know their destinations on a daily basis or are they taking off without any clue as to where they are going?

After developing an awareness of your strengths in your natural state, and gaining rapport with your coachee, the next important step is **Stipulate**.

Your ability to elicit specific objectives from people is crucial to your success and during every coaching interaction we must clarify and focus on that objective with a coachee.

This chapter offers you fast and effective tools and tips that enable you to do this every time.

## The Importance of developing Habits that increase your Personal Focus

Who do you know that sits in front of the television in the evening thinking that it relaxes them, and finds themselves watching something that they are not even interested in? What if this person's passion was golf, and a trip to the driving range allowed them to relax even more and take their mind completely off the day's events? If your objective this evening were to completely and utterly relax, what would you do that would guarantee this result? Every time you take action, ask yourself what outcome are you holding in mind?

Rather than leave the future to chance, have specific outcomes for yourself across every area of your life. Action without knowing where you are going may well be a waste of time. Be clear on what you want and you will know automatically what you need to do.

It should be an ingrained habit that you pin down a specific outcome before entering into action planning with yourself and your coachees. This can be done within seconds. The more you ask what the objectives are, the more you condition yourself and others to be thinking in this way on a daily basis.

## Are you and your Coachee aiming for the same Target?

If I ask a dozen people to describe the first picture that comes to mind when they hear the words "sailing ships", I guarantee they would all have their own interpretations of what "sailing ships" means to them.

**Stipulate** is your chance to ensure that your thoughts about objectives are aligned with those of the coachee. Ensuring you are on the same wavelength as the coachee is vital when coaching, as our subsequent coaching and questions will miss the mark.

When a coachee shares their objective with me I use their language patterns to clarify exactly what they mean. If I don't then I am in danger of putting my own picture in the frame, making assumptions and creating something in my mind that is not what the coachee wants.

A great tip is to write down the goal and circle it at every opportunity to keep each coaching interaction fully focused.

If I need clarification as to what they mean then I ask them more detailed questions using the following goal setting models.

## Goal-setting Models that guarantee Success

It is pointless creating new goal setting models when some of the simplest and most overlooked models work so well! If you have seen these before, then I encourage you to go over them again and ask yourself how disciplined and effective you are in using them.

**SMART Objectives -** Every goal <u>must</u> meet all five criteria.

| | |
|---|---|
| **Specific** | Know exactly what you are aiming for |
| **Measurable** | Make it a quantitative measure every time |
| **Agreed** | Always have complete agreement with the coachee |
| **Realistic** | Be sure that the goal can be achieved |
| **Timed** | Always commit to a deadline |

You may have come across a similar model that suggests the 'A' stands for 'Achievable'. In my opinion, Achievable means the same as Realistic and therefore the model is even more powerful when objectives are 'Agreed to'.

I also like to use this more advanced version of SMART objectives especially when coaching people towards business objectives because it is so important that the goals meet the needs of the business and are in line with positive human values that strengthen team performance.

| | |
|---|---|
| **Specific** | Know exactly what you are aiming for |
| **Measurable** | Make it a quantitative measure every time |
| **Agreed** | Always have complete agreement with the coachee |
| **Realistic** | Be sure that the goal can be achieved |
| **Timed** | Always commit to a deadline |
| **Ethical** | The goal must be in the best interests of others |
| **Relevant** | The goal must always meet the needs of the business |

**PROOF EXERCISE**

Research proves that on average it takes 21 days to form a habit so this one is an absolute must if you are serious about being a coach. Commit to setting and finishing three specific outcomes everyday for 21 days using these models.

This is not the same as making a 'to do' list; "actions" are not "objectives", so make sure your objectives are compelling and give you that sense of achievement by the end of the day.

**Producing a Statement of an achievable Outcome**

This NLP model is by far the most effective of goal setting models and can be used in the context of forming business and personal objectives. It works by produces outcomes that are in line with a person's values making it natural for them to feel motivated and inspired to take action.

What's the difference between a goal and an outcome?

Goals are often described in quite general terms. For example, 'I want to introduce a good coaching culture into my organisation' or 'I want my team to understand each other'. Neither of these objectives are described with any specificity.

This is where the following outcome-oriented model comes in. An outcome represents a goal that has been developed to a point where it becomes quite clear what actually needs to be done to achieve it. The chances of the objective being reached are thus much higher.

With practice you will find you can deliver the whole process in around two minutes. Alternatively, give the coachee a copy of the questions and ask them to take a few moments to answer them and come back to you when they have finished.

1. <u>Stated in the positive.</u>
   What specifically do you want?
2. <u>Specify present situation.</u>
   Where are you now?
3. <u>Specify outcome.</u>
   What will you see, hear, feel, etc., when you have it?
4. <u>Specify evidence procedure.</u>
   How will you know when you have it?
5. <u>Is it congruently desirable?</u>
   What will this outcome get for you or allow you to do?
6. <u>Is it self-initiated and self-maintained?</u>
   Is it only for you?
7. <u>Is it appropriately contextualized?</u>
   Where, when, how, and with who do you want it?
8. <u>What resources are needed?</u>
   What do you have now, and what do you need to get your outcome?
   Have you ever done this before?
   Do you know anyone who has already achieved this?
   Can you act as if you have it?
9. <u>Is it ecological?</u>
   No one exists in isolation; what are the consequences of achieving your outcome in the wider context? Would you have to give up anything, or take on anything?

For what purpose do you want this?

What will you gain or lose if you have it?

What will happen if you get it?
What won't happen if you get it?
What will happen if you don't get it?
What won't happen if you don't get it?

**PROOF EXERCISE**

Think of something you want to achieve, be it a personal or business objective and work through the model questions and allow yourself to see how powerful this can be.

Use this model now to clarify with yourself at least 6 objectives and practice using this model on a daily basis.

## Using this Model effectively to coach a Team

In meetings, use breakout sessions to clarify and agree goals with everyone in your team. Always make sure that everyone has reached a consensus to the answers given for each question.

Remember when group coaching, one of your objectives is to inspire *everyone* in the team, not just one or two people. Be aware of situations where one or more people take over answering the questions on behalf of the group.

In government, not everyone in the cabinet agrees with all of the decisions all of the time; but once a majority decision has been reached the agreement within the cabinet is that everyone stands by that decision, no matter what. Maybe such a principle in a business environment would help to make goal-setting a quicker and more effective process?

## Handling Emotional Resistance when goal setting

Each Enneagram type can sometime experience challenges in goals setting when operating from the average to unhealthy aspects of their type.

Here is a list of what you may notice when goal setting with each of them:

**ONES**        May strive for unrealistic perfection in terms of the result rather than being happy or forgiving of small imperfections

**TWOS**        May have an excessive focus on the goals being good for others as opposed to themselves

**THREES**      May go for a goal that 'looks good' in front of others rather than something they truly want

**FOURS**       May strive for something that makes them completely unique from others rather than the ordinary

**FIVES**       May go for a goal more that further increases their knowledge rather than apply what they already know towards a new goal

**SIXES**       May prefer to be given direction rather than take responsibility for deciding for themselves what the goal should be; or may
prefer a team-focused goal rather than an individual one.

**SEVENS**      May find it difficult to focus on one or two areas, seeking a wide variety of experiences rather than apply their attention and energy to one specific outcome

**EIGHTS**      May choose a goal that is important to them without considering it's impact on other people

**NINES**       May find it easier to decide what they don't want rather than take a position on what they do want

What do you do when someone cannot decide exactly what he or she wants? It happens. Few people take time to decide exactly what they want.

Asking, "what exactly do you want to achieve?" can sometimes result in the answer "I don't know". As a searching question, it can sometimes cause emotional turmoil and resistance making it difficult for you to move forward.

This is often the case with the type **NINE** in the Enneagram. **NINES** have been conditioned over the years not to feel comfortable in asking for what they want. Their strategy is to keep themselves small and put other peoples' needs before their own AND they can often identify more easily with what they don't want rather than what they do want.

Conditioning over a number of years has made people many feel uncomfortable about asking for what they want. The Enneagram highlights motivational reasons why this is so for *certain types.*

**TWOS** Learn that asking for something for themselves is selfish and feel very uncomfortable focusing on their own needs
**FIVES** Learn to feel safe in the private world of their mind and often intellectualize the process instead of understanding what their heart truly desires.
**NINES** Learn to merge with the agendas of others and believe that their desires are not important enough.

In the event of a 'don't know' response to the question "what do you want?" the following questions will be of use to you.

"Well if you did know, what would it be?"
"What would be your best suggestion/guess?"
"What if there were no limits, then what would you want?"
"In an ideal world, what do you want?"
"Tell me what you don't want and then we can work back to what you do want."

If you still have no answer and you feel the temptation to tell your coachee what their outcome might be, or offer suggestions, then don't. All you will be doing is reinforcing this behaviour. Your role lies in empowering them to make decisions for the good of themselves, the people around them and maybe even the organisation.

Giving a person a little more time and space often helps, because the answer will come to them  - often when they least expect it.

So, why not ask them to come back to you with their thoughts a little later?

## How to increase Confidence when the Objective appears to overwhelm the Coachee

A feeling of being overwhelmed hinders performance and can quickly destroy self-esteem. If you have mastered 'Relating' to your coachee, you will now be sensitive enough to notice when your coachee feels that the goal is not achievable.

Only move forward when your coachee is 100% congruent in his/her belief that the objective is achievable and is indeed committed to taking the action.

Often all it takes is to break the goal down into a number of manageable steps, and focus on them one at a time. Setting mini goals, which lead to the achievement of the overall key objective, is a strategy used by sales managers to focus individuals on more manageable targets on a daily basis.

Treat each one of those mini-objectives as an individual coaching process and ensure that they each meet relevant goal-setting criteria. After coaching for some time, both you and the coachee become familiar with this mini goal-setting approach. Keep fully consistent with your approach and then your coachee will be equally so with their behaviour.

## Aligning the Objectives to meet the Needs of the Business and the Individual

It is possible to agree objectives that inspire people and take into account more of their personal desires. This guarantees more success for the individual, the team and the organisation.

With practice, you can use the goals setting models as a template from which to create your own questions that align the objectives to meet the needs of the individual AND the business.

Here are examples of carefully phrased questions that allow the coachee to search for objectives that satisfy both the business needs and more of their personal desires:

*Where does the focus for you need to be in order to enjoy this project and help exceed the current needs of the business?*

*What objectives can we agree now that will benefit both yourself and the business?*

*What specific business targets interest you the most?*

*What would you want to take into account when agreeing objectives with your team?*

At first you may want to consider carefully the questions that allow you to do this in the context of your people and the business needs. With practice you will find yourself creating questions 'in the moment' that focus on what everyone wants in the team.


**PROOF EXERCISE**

Spend 15 minutes every day brainstorming and designing questions that align the needs of the individual with the needs of the business.


**Measuring the Immeasurable**

Improvement in behaviours and attitudes is often considered difficult to measure and yet a very simple way of doing so is to use a subjective scale of 1-10 to measure the perceived level of skills and knowledge in a chosen area.

By doing so, coachees can quantify and acknowledge within themselves the improvements they make over time as well as benefit from an internal sense that progress has been made.

And, from the coach's point of view, this simple method provides further evidence that your coaching is improving the skills and attributes within your team.

Let us take presentation skills as an example.

John (Coach):        "On a scale of 1-10, how confident do you feel delivering presentations?"

Sam (coachee):       "Between 5 and 6."

John (Coach):        "Where would you like to be by the end of this month?"

Sam (Coachee):       "I would like to be at least an 8."

John (Coachee):      "Great. What specifically will you see, hear and feel by the end of the month, that would let you know you had increased your confidence levels to 8?"

Sam (Coachee):       I would be able to stand in front of a group, using my slides effectively, I would rarely need to look at my notes and I would be feeling happier about the presentation that is coming up next month.

Their perception as to where they are is what counts – your opinion does not. Only by truly acknowledging where they are now can they know internally what they must take responsibility for.

These questions will help you to guide your coaches in establishing a scale and benchmark.

"Where do you feel you are right now on a scale of 1-10, 10 being great?"
"Where would you like to be by the end of the day?"
"What do you need to focus on to make that happen for you?"

I use this scale with groups and individuals during our training events. Setting the agenda this way at the beginning of each programme encourages participants to take responsibility for their own personal development. It also serves to highlight the most important elements of the programme to focus on how to get maximum value and benefit from the day.

At the middle and end of the day I can review where they are and ensure they have achieved what they wanted from the programme. I also check they can actually see for themselves an improvement in their awareness and skill levels. This is what builds momentum and gives them permission to acknowledge to themselves that they have improved.

**Summary for Stipulate**

**Three most important Things to remember:**

1. Always make sure that your goals and objectives meet one of the goal- setting criteria of either the SMART, SMARTER or keys to achievable outcome models.

2. Your coaching questions are more effective when you are certain that you and the coachee are aiming for the same target.

3. Measure everything. Use a scale of 1-10 if you cannot quantify the objective.

# Chapter Eight

Evaluate:
Identifying the 'Real' Performance Blocks and Gaps

> *"Awareness is perceiving things as they really are; self-awareness is recognizing those internal factors that distort one's own perception of reality. Most people think that they are objective, but absolute objectivity does not exist. The best we have is degrees of it, but the closer we manage to get to it the better."*
>
> **John Whitmore**

## Where are you now in relation to where you want to be?

Once the goal has been clarified, we can move on to explore the coachee's current situation and perceptions of reality. This will encourage him/her to think about what is preventing the achievement of this goal and the most effective way to bridge the gap between where they are now and where they want to be.

Objectivity is vital and here you can make good use of what is known in NLP as the Meta model - a priceless tool to maintain emotional detachment, remove judgement from your coaching and communicate with greater clarity. I highly recommend using this tool. Full details can be found later in this chapter.

The **EVALUATE** step may overlap with the next coaching step which is to motivate your coachee. It does not matter. For the purposes of this model I would like to separate the process, but remember there is no right or wrong order in which the questions need to be asked. All we are doing is giving you an abundance of strategies to use at the appropriate time.

**Why this Step alone will always improve Performance.**

This step of the coaching process raises the awareness of the coachee to such a high level that often no further coaching is necessary, because the root causes and problems uncovered can be easily overcome with slight adjustment.

Imagine a satellite dish that has been knocked two centimetres off to the right causing the transmitted signal to miss the target by many miles. A slight adjustment can put the signal bang on target. A slight adjustment in this context is a well placed question.

Evaluate coaching questions can be as simple as this:

Where are you now?
What is the situation now with regard to this objective?
What have you completed already?
What actions have you taken so far?
What have been the effects of this action?
What do you already know?
What has the performance been to date?
What results do you already have?
What is going well for you right now?
What actions have you taken exactly/already?
What appears to be getting in the way?
What are you doing at the moment?

## What is preventing your Coachee from moving forward?

Behind every reason given by a coachee for not having what they want, or not being where they want to be, or not having achieved the objective, there may be a negative thought or belief – whether about himself or herself, other people and / or the overall situation in question.

Once this block is uncovered the coachee has a choice: either to hold onto that thought or belief, change it or just let it go.

By helping them to let go or change these beliefs a great coach opens their mind to the opportunity and the possibility that they can indeed take responsibility and take action.

Questions such as:

What is really preventing you right now from having what you really want?
What is stopping you from achieving this objective?
What is the holdback in taking this action?
Do you know that to be absolutely true?
What if you had made them up as a result of your life experience?
Who would you be without this thought or belief?
What would you be capable of without this thought or belief?

Subconscious beliefs are what drive much of our behaviour. If a person is not happy with the results they are getting, or not living up to their true capacity, then a coach plays a valuable role in allowing the coachee to uncover them and gain a new perspective on these perceived blocks. This moves them closer to the healthy aspect of their Enneagram type, into greater awareness, naturally and increases their sense of personal responsibility.

Some of the beliefs derive from painful past experiences. These are just memories and having nothing to do with what is actually happening right here and now. Some memories are so painful that we block them out of our awareness altogether. You can assist then coachee in finding out what they are to uncover the belief that is holding them back.

## The Question behind the Question

An important point to be aware of when coaching is that all too often people will attempt to avoid the first question. You can observe this in a number of ways. The person you are coaching may either:

Lie to you
Close down
Change the subject
Answer a different question altogether

Your coachee may not be aware of the real reason he/she is not following through with their objectives. It is very important that you uncover the deeper, unconscious levels of resistance in order to make progress with them.

Before writing this book, I was experiencing some resistance to starting the project. I sought coaching from someone I knew would be courageous enough to keep questioning me to uncover what was really holding me back.

Sanjay is such a dear friend and I love working with him because even if I am getting angry at his questions he keeps persisting. He focuses on blowing away the deepest limiting beliefs that are holding me back and never allows me to get away with giving superficial answers.

In this particular case, my superficial reasons included, "I do not have the patience", "I have never written a book before", "I do not have time."

Then he said to me, "Come on Anne, what is the real reason?"
"Fear of failure", I said,
"And anything else? " said Sanjay
"Yes, fear of success."

It all became so clear to me in an instant. My head was saying 'yes, write the book ', but my subconscious was resisting and pulling me in all directions.

Just the awareness itself instantly created a change, as I started to laugh at the thought of what I was putting myself through. It was at this point that I knew what I had to do.

It takes a courageous and caring coach to ask the question that uncovers the truth, but when they do then they really make a difference to people's lives. When we admit the truth, we know even more about what must happen to change the situation.

The more people get to know and trust me as a coach, the quicker I can go straight to the golden question; "What's really behind this?"

## The Meta Model

The NLP Meta Model is one of the most effective questioning tools I have come across. It provides a framework within which you can get to the real truth, which is preventing someone from moving forward. I highly recommend you take time to learn and apply these tools.

Much of our daily conversation consists of wild generalisations, assumptions and vagueness. If someone can tell you specifically what is bothering him or her, or what's getting in the way of achieving an outcome, then you can help him or her deal with it. If they just use vague language, and project confusion and uncertainty, you become as lost as they are in their mental fog.

As a coach you have to be aware of this fog that obscures good communication and be ready with some sharp questioning skills to light the way to some sense.

The model is designed specifically to raise people's awareness of their language patterns and uncover the truth behind the statements they make.

**Generalisations**

By becoming generally more aware of the nuances of language when you communicate, you will notice how the generalisations made by the coachee point to limiting belief systems and emotional barriers which block access to their natural talents and abilities.

The following examples of generalisations are followed by suggestions for your response as a coach. Each question is designed to uncover the true cause of the performance block and gives you an opportunity to reframe their meaning, and creating lasting change.

| Statement | Coach's Response |
| --- | --- |
| "I am always making mistakes." "I never get it right." | Always? Never? |
| "I have to achieve these targets!" | "What will happen if you don't achieve these targets?" "What would happen if you did achieve these target?" |
| " I just can't do this!" | "What would happen if you did?" "What is preventing you from doing this?" |
| "I have to train these people fully." | What would happen if you did train them fully? "What would happen if you didn't?" |

## Distortions

Too often we inaccurately represent situations in the way we describe, generalise or theorise about our experiences.

It is so easy to distort the truth and your coachee will be doing this for a good reason. However, if this distortion is not helping them be where they want to be, we can turn the situation around and use these questions to bring more truth to the situation and encourage them to take more responsibility for themselves.

Let us take a closer look at how we distort the truth and what questions we can ask to uncover opportunities and change a person's perception.

| Statement | Coach's Response |
| --- | --- |
| "The team doesn't like me." | "How do you know the team doesn't like you?"<br>(Uncovers the source of the issue) |
| "It's not right to cut costs." | "Who says it's not right to cut costs?"<br>(Creates ownership)<br>"How do you know it's not right?"<br>(Uncovers their beliefs) |
| "The manager is making me work long hours; he doesn't like me. | "How does his making you work long hours mean he doesn't like you?" |

| | |
|---|---|
| "I feel angry when I am not told about things that are going on." | "How does not being told make you choose to feel angry?"<br><br>It is an interesting thought that at some level we choose to feel the way we do about situations, people and circumstances.<br><br>By uncovering beliefs people have about themselves, you have an opportunity to offer them a different perspective and change the way they feel for the better. |
| "If he knew how hard we were all working he wouldn't do that." | "How do you know he doesn't know?" |

## Deletions

Deletions make it easy for us to forget valuable information that can transform our performance. Being aware of this, you can bring the coachee's awareness around to what can be a vital missing part of the jigsaw.

Use the following response questions to uncover ideas within and create an empowering reality for the person you are coaching.

| Statement | Coach's Response |
|---|---|
| "There is no teamwork in this office." | "How would you like the teamwork to be?"<br>(Uncovers their expectations and enables you to manage them.) |

| | |
|---|---|
| "He ignored my ideas" | "How specifically?" |
| "She did not do what I asked" | "What specifically didn't she do?" |
| "I am not very happy about this." | "About what, specifically?" |
| "The team never listen to me" | "Who in the team does not listen to you?" |
| "She is a much better sales person." | "Compared to whom?" |
| | "Compared to what?" |
| "This is a better team" | |

(Also applies to words such as, more, worse, less and least)

## TOP TIP

When using the Meta Model, pay attention to the context in which statements are being made and not the content. It will allow you maintain more of your natural state. If you feel yourself becoming emotionally entangled and defensive over people's responses then take a breath, drop your attention to your feet, regroup and then continue.

You will find further suggested questions listed at the end of each chapter, relating to the various steps in the coaching model.

### Knowing when to move on to the next Coaching Step

Rather like a pile of stacking plates that you see in a canteen, (where each plate that is picked up is replaced by one that springs up from underneath it), you may use this method to quickly uncover several blocks one at a time. The first time I ever used the Meta Model with a coaching partner we continued questioning for over thirty minutes, when in fact the root cause of the problem had been uncovered within the first two or three minutes.

Here are some signals to look out for that tell you it's time to move your coaching along:

- When you can sense that they are full taking responsibility for their behaviour and beginning to search inside of themselves for ways in which they can solve the problem for themselves.
- The moment you find your coachee giving you similar answers to different questions then you know there is nothing more behind the answers they are giving.
- The 'ah hah' moment when their eyes light up and they realise how their thoughts and beliefs have been driving their behaviour. Their eyes often widen, their breathing and body language become more relaxed.
- When they are asking you what they can do about it.
- When you have a significant limiting belief to work on that will improve a person's ability to achieve the result (see the chapter on 'Motivate', to learn how to transform limiting beliefs).

**Summary for Evaluate**

**Three most important Things to remember:**

1. It can be as simple as increasing the coachee's awareness as to where they are now in terms of where they want to be.

2. Investigate and uncover the limiting beliefs or thoughts that are holding them back. These will be the ones they are least aware of.

3. Learn and use the Meta Model – it's a tool for life!

# Chapter Nine

## Motivate

> "Keep away from people who try to belittle your ambitions. Small people always do that, but the really great ones make you feel that you too, can become great."
>
> **Mark Twain**

When you are coaching, do the people you work with have sufficiently compelling reasons for springing into action and doing whatever it takes to achieve the goal?

When you want to inspire people, do you say things that you know will motivate you, instead of truly understanding what will naturally motivate them?

Can you always find the drive and commitment inside yourself that gives you the resources you need to achieve your goals in life, no matter what happens to you?

The Motivate step is all about helping your coachees discover those reasons that connect them with their driving emotions as much as possible, allowing them to naturally overcome any resistance to actions necessary to achieve a result.

We make decisions for emotional reasons and justify them with logic. When coaching, pay attention to how your coachee is feeling. Ask yourself whether those feelings are strong enough to guarantee they will do whatever it takes to achieve the goal. In other words, are they speaking to you from their heart or from their head?

Logic will not motivate, but strong heartfelt emotion will. Your experience will tell you when a person means what they say and they are speaking from their heart and not their head. So, for you to know whether or not you are motivating a person you also need to be open to your own feelings.

For some coaches, inspiring people by drawing upon their true enthusiasm and willingness to really go for a target is the greatest test. Conscious thoughts often disguise our true feelings.

Have the courage to use coaching questions which reveal people's true feelings and change their perspective or beliefs about what is possible, so that it changes how they feel.

Are you willing to ask whatever questions it takes to allow them to get in touch with the <u>emotional reasons</u> to get the results <u>they want</u>?

You could say that your role as a coach is to facilitate the process of selling the concept to both the coachee's conscious and subconscious mind. The perceived benefits of taking action must significantly outweigh any other reason they have for not following through.

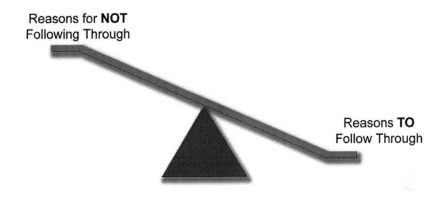

Reasons for **NOT** Following Through

Reasons **TO** Follow Through

Change happens quickly when you can change how people feel. Until that point is reached your coachee will continue with the behaviour which feels most comfortable.

By connecting your coachees to how they truly feel and helping them use these feelings to create compelling and innovative solutions, you engage their entire nervous system. You are involving their subconscious mind, the part of them that needs the most convincing before the activity becomes automatic and purely self-driven, without any conscious need for willpower. Some people are more in touch with their feelings than others, but we all have them.

Always remember that what motivates you is not necessarily what motivates other people. Forgetting this important point is the most common mistake managers make when they want to increase motivation and morale within their team. Only by paying 100% attention to how your coachee reacts will you know if you are moving in the right direction. If you get it wrong, then your coaching can be a waste of time.

And never underrate the importance of your own motivation levels at all times. Unless you can bring a strong and positive mindset every time to the people you are coaching, your effectiveness in using Results Coaching in 60 Seconds will be limited. So it is absolutely vital that you master the art of self-motivation, to quickly overcome challenges and set a good example to your coachees.

Use coaching questions and strategies demonstrated in this chapter to give the coachee more compelling and emotional reasons for committing to this goal.

**Values**

Our values tell us what is most important to us in business and indeed in life. We already have subconsciously prioritised our values, based on our life experience to-date. The order of these values can change overnight, however, if we experience a significant emotional event such as the sudden death of a loved one, when instantly our family may become more important to us.

Money is a value, but it is what we call a 'means' value. How the money makes a person feel is known as the 'ends' value. This distinction between two types of apparently linked values relates directly to discovering what feelings people prefer to experience on a daily basis.

For you as a coach, knowing, understanding and then utilising your coachee's personal 'ends values' is a powerful tool, which will strike at their very core.

The following lists show examples of means and what their ends values may be

| Means Values – what is important | Ends Values – what the value delivers |
| --- | --- |
| Money | Freedom, security, control |
| Health | Well-being, relaxed |
| Relationships | Love, connection |
| Family | Love and connection |

Remember these are different for each individual and so getting to know what is important to every single coachee is one of your priorities as a coach.

If you are attempting, for instance, to motivate a staff member by pointing out how secure their job is, and their highest value is "connection with people", then you may wish to change your approach and shift the job security emphasis to one which highlights the benefits of working and getting along as a team. By doing so you are touching what is far more important to them and they will respond positively.


## PROOF EXERCISE

Spend a day asking the people you are coaching what is most important to them and if they give you a 'means' value, ask what it would ultimately give them. If they answer with another 'means' value ask how *that* would ultimately make them feel.

Make a list of these 'ends' values for the people you are coaching and utilise them regularly.

## Using the Enneagram to motivate

The Enneagram exposes our values and therefore what drives the way we work, how we make decisions, how we see ourselves, and how we relate to people. It is a beautifully elegant tool for recognising the different types of motivations that underlie our behaviour.

Let us take another look at an overview of the core motivations of each Enneagram type:

**Perfectionist –**   Wants to get things right
**Carer -**   Wants to help others
**Achiever -**   Want to experience success
**Artist -**   Want to explore their feelings and be unique
**Genius -**   Want objective information
**Loyalist -**   Want to feel safe
**Adventurer -**   Want to experience a variety of things in life
**Leader -**   Want to be in control
**Peacemaker -**   Want to merge and connect with others

An understanding of these values as a coach means that you can tailor your coaching questions to suit the core values and motivations of your coachees. By meeting these values on a daily basis they will naturally feel motivated to take action.

It stands to reason that you would not motivate a 'Carer' using the same strategies as you would for a Thinker!

And if you only ever coach people using your own personal set of values or Enneagram type motivations as a guide to what 'should' motivate others, then your coaching will clearly be compromised.


## Strategies for motivating each Enneagram Type

You should by now have identified the different types of people you are coaching and agreed this type identification with them, you can use the following information as an indicator of their core motivation and therefore their values.

You are provided with business case studies, where people tell you from their own perspective how they prefer to be coached and therefore motivated. Remember they are operating from the average to unhealthy aspects of their profile and these tips are designed to help you to move them into the healthy aspects as quickly as possible.

Once again these principles can be used for business, life coaching and yes – family coaching, for friends and family!

You will also find strategies as to how to coach each type quickly and effectively. Pay particular attention to your own type and practice using these strategies to coach and motivate yourself!

# THE PERFECTIONIST
## CASE STUDY

James works as Project Manager for a construction company.

"My Line Manager, Bob, is a nice guy and we get on well together. He is always on time for the meetings we have and he keeps all of the commitments he makes to me. He is polite, fair and honest. I like that in someone; after all a 'thank you' or 'you're welcome' goes a long way with me and good etiquette is hard to come by these days."

"I prefer a structured approach when being coached. There is nothing worse than someone going off at a tangent. Keep coaching concise and I really like having a written action plan. Such agreements mean people will nearly always follow through, having made such a definite commitment."

"Of course, I am always right! Well, I like to think so anyway. If you want to challenge my opinions without getting angry with me, use a 'what if' approach to give me a different perspective and open me up to more options.

Because I focus so much on getting things just right, I usually know before anybody else if I have made a mistake or done something wrong. Getting criticised for the mistake just makes me feel a whole lot worse, because I do a pretty good job of beating myself up anyway."

"I can spot mistakes immediately and will forgive you if you admit these and apologise for making them. In fact, this gesture will allow me to feel more comfortable with you as making mistakes is one of the things I am most afraid of. You see, I have a natural tendency to focus on what is wrong rather than what is right."

"When I become 'picky' I may annoy people, I know, but whilst I often justify my point of view using logic, I am actually motivated by a deep desire to make things works for the good of everyone."

"I hate being interrupted or coached without being asked if it is convenient or if I am having a bad day. It's best to ask my permission first. Better still, tell me a joke or make me laugh. I am at my best when I am having fun.

"Showing anger can be highly inappropriate and therefore on a difficult day I rarely tell people how I am feeling. It's more important to keep control in these situations, although if you can find out what is really bothering me and make me feel comfortable in expressing my true feelings, it often releases built up pressure that causes me stress. Don't take things personally, just allow me to let off some steam."

"I can be great fun to work with and like being made to laugh. It's good for me to take regular 5-minute breaks and take physical exercise in the evening when I go home. I learned that I am considerably more relaxed when I take regular exercise, apparently it has something to do with my type being connected to that of the '**SEVEN**', the adventurer."

"Taking a playful approach to life allows me to be more creative with new ideas and more open to the opinions of others people. Just be authentic and straight with me and acknowledge my achievements occasionally, and we will get on fine."

## What ONES want

- To do a job correctly
- Quality performance
- To improve the current situation
- To treat people fairly and be treated fairly
- Facts
- Precision
- Clear operational procedures
- Vision
- To put things right!
- Things in the correct order

## Top Coaching Tips for ONES

- Encourage them to take breaks
- Use written agreements regularly
- Allow then to show their anger and let off steam without judging them
- Use a structured approach
- **ONES** have a very strong internal frame of reference so make sure you allow them to make their own decisions
- Ask questions around practical solutions
- Be very specific
- Be punctual with them

# THE CARER
# CASE STUDY

Sally is House Keeping Managing in a Leisure Resort

"Providing people spend a little time with me face-to-face I can keep myself motivated for relatively long periods of time."

"It has taken some time for me to be comfortable with being coached. I naturally prefer coaching other people and it used to make me feel uncomfortable having someone focus their attention on me. Tim, the Resort Manager has to remind me who is coaching whom, because apparently I have this habit of turning the conversation around to coaching him! Allow me to coach you in return occasionally – we love to help!"

"I can tell when a person is being false with me and that makes me very uncomfortable."

"Help me to enjoy work even more by making sure that whatever I am doing I am interacting with other people and show me the bigger picture when agreeing objectives, as this is how my mind prefers to work"

"Being taken for granted annoys me the most and if you are not careful I will find subtle ways of seeking revenge - just use this a signal to pay them a little more attention. I once intentionally forgot to send an email to someone because all they ever did was ask for things on a daily basis without giving anything back."

"I know I like to be liked and it does hurt when people become angry with me. I hate sarcasm too. I prefer people to spend a little time with me face-to-face. It's more personal, don't you think?"

"Small gifts for each other are great to say thank you and I do this for my team occasionally. It's the personal touch that makes the difference."

"I am at my best when I can serve people and I will do almost anything for you if I know that you like me."

## What TWOS want

- To feel welcome and to make others feel welcome
- To help and support people
- To focus on the needs of other people
- To be liked and recognised by others for making a difference to them
- To be loved
- To deliver and receive good customer service

## Top Coaching Tips for TWOS

- Use a face-to-face approach when coaching wherever possible
- Focus on how what they want to achieve can help others
- Find solutions that both serve people and meet the needs of the business at the same time.
- **TWOS** like to look at the big picture so use your coaching questions to focus them in this way
- Give them personal rewards on a regular basis

# THE ACHIEVER
# CASE STUDY

Alison is Marketing Director for a computer software company.

"I used to be too busy for coaching but this 60 second coaching is great for me because I like it when people get straight to the point. Interruptions annoy me greatly. They slow me down. So when I am busy working I always say it's best to catch me in between tasks rather than in the middle of something."

"Warm-ups are helpful but should be brief. Too much touchy/feely stuff doesn't usually work either, but direct, positive enthusiastic statements that emphasise impact on bottom line and a focus on what I need or want usually goes a very long way."

"I love being challenged at work, although I often put too much pressure on myself by over-committing to people. This often means I am working very early in the morning and late into the evening to get things done."

"Give me short-term plans as I tend to get bored with long-term projects. Anything short-term I will fly through and really enjoy achieving success on a daily basis."

"Many people in the office are negative and seem to look on the downside of everything. That's why I always go to see Mark for my coaching because he is always upbeat and positive. He makes me feel good about myself. Coming up from being a clerk in the office many years ago to Director now, he says how proud he is of the things I have done and how much he enjoys coaching me"

"He is very smart because he sees how I rush into things. Encouraging me to slow down has produced better results for me even if it feels uncomfortable sometimes."

"I am very competitive and so do not respond well to people whom I perceive as being in competition with me. To avoid getting yourself into difficulty with me, use collaborative techniques. I then understand how my efforts are contributing to the team goal."

## What THREES want

- Success
- To be perceived as the best
- Material wealth
- To work efficiently to get results
- To pursue goals
- To use a practical approach to get things done
- Results as quickly as possible
- Status

## Top Coaching Tips for THREES

- Coach them quickly and with full enthusiasm for their goals
- Praise their confidence, energy and enthusiasm regularly.
- Avoid getting into competition with them
- Use challenges, status and profile strategies to motivate them
- Short-term plans and objectives work well
- Encourage them occasionally to slow down and relax.
- Show them how they can be the 'first' to do something
- Use status to motivate them

# THE ARTIST
# CASE STUDY

Kieran works as a graphic designer for an advertising company.

"Being a sensitive person I prefer a gentler approach to coaching. I have a tendency to panic when put under pressure."

"Kathy is great because she listens to my crazy ideas and never dismisses any of them. She takes her time when coaching me and knows that I work well when I can really allow my creative juices to flow. My intuition always tells me what will work and what won't."

"There are a lot of designers in the company and we are all very different. Kath makes each one of us feel special and values the unique talents we bring to the company. None of us like the team coaching approach, we much prefer the one-to-one contact and working on our own to bring the personal touch to what we do."

"My previous manager used to tell me what to do and how to do it. I came very close to resigning my position. I chose this role to be able to use my creative talents and I felt I was not being allowed to use them."

## What FOURS want

- To be different, unique and special
- To use their feelings and emotions to communicate with themselves and others
- To find even more creative ways of getting things done
- To sound out people's feelings

- To avoid doing 'ordinary' work
- To like things to be aesthetically pleasing
- To enjoy acquiring special skills

## Top Coaching Tips for FOURS

- Inspire them to use their creative talents
- Accept their ideas without judgement
- Putting them under pressure will only increase their emotional resistance and hinder performance
- Encourage them to use their intuition

# THE GENIUS
# CASE STUDY

Jeremy is a computer programmer.

"I have been interested in computers since the age of 6 and even now spend all of my spare time on my pc. People used to see me as a bit of a nerd at school."

"I get on well with my boss. He took the time to get to know me, not like my old manager who would just question me all of the time as if I didn't know my job. I like the fact that it takes him only a few moments to ask me questions that allow me to further expand my knowledge and he never coaches me in front of other people."

"I like working on my own but there are a few people I spend more time talking with. These people are really friendly and accept me for who I am. I like helping them sort out their computer problems."

"We **FIVES** are small chunk information sorters with a strong internal frame of reference. This means we will make up our own mind based on the way we put the facts and pieces of information together and it is better to allow us to do so."

"The worst thing someone can do is not give me space and help me to feel safe in my environment."

## What FIVES want

- To analyse problems and situations
- To be 'observers' of what is going on.
- To be experts in one particular area
- To learn about new insights and thinking skills
- Time to reflect before taking action
- To often work and be by themselves
- To work in quiet areas with preferably a minimum of social contact.
- Rational and critical thinking

## Top Coaching Tips for FIVES

- **FIVES** like structure and will feel safe with you if you use the same coaching process with them.
- Pay special attention when you notice them doing something without being asked and thank them for it.
- Seek ways of helping them to develop their expertise even further

## THE LOYALIST
## CASE STUDY

David is Sales Manager for an insurance company

"Results Coaching in 60 Seconds is great for me! When being coached by someone who is quick enough at asking me the questions then I come out with the answers without analysing them or the situation. It's funny really because I always know what to do. I just find myself doubting and questioning sometimes to make sure it's the right decision."

"I prefer if you admit to me if you feel uncomfortable or have made a mistake. I want to help people and be part of the team. I relax more when I know it's ok to want security and it helps to know that you want security too when you are coaching me."

"It took some time to get to trust my boss and he knows that it's a good idea to keep building that trust everyday. You see I find it hard to forgive people, once someone has been untrustworthy I find it difficult to fully trust them again."

"As for Sarah, my old boss, she would flatter me all of the time and I just knew that she wanted something from me."

"We should always explore the positives and the negatives because then we know we can make a decision that is the safer option."

## What SIXES want

- To contribute to the 'team effort'
- To work with trustworthy people
- To be trusted
- Security
- Customary and established ways of working
- To work with reliable people
- Commitment
- To develop relationships

## Top Coaching Tips for SIXES

- Be straight and to the point when coaching. The faster the better with a **SIX**
- Limit compliments – they think you want something even if you don't!!
- Allow them to explore the positives and the negatives.
- Never say, "don't worry" to a **SIX** – it is part of their nature and it may cause them to worry even more.
- Encourage them to trust and develop confidence in their own decisions.
- Be certain they have a clear plan as to what to do.
- They naturally prefer to be led rather than to lead because leadership carries with it too much responsibility. Make sure they take responsibility for action plans.
- Acknowledge their concerns authentically and ask questions such as "What do you think you should do?" to turn a negative situation around.

## THE ENTHUSIAST
## CASE STUDY

Mike is a fitness instructor

"My boss has learned to spend a few moments with me at the beginning of each day to focus my attention on what needs to be finished before the day is done. These guidelines have to be really clear and concise for me or I will find ways to distract myself. His coaching is fun and fast which is just the way I like it!"

"The vision we have for the fitness centre really excites me. Although some days I do need reminding regularly, to inspire me to keep going."

"I have a great friend who reminds me of all the good things I have in my life and how far I have come when I am having a 'down' day. He tells me when he is having a bad day too and I find it easy to cheer him up!"


## What SEVENS want

- A variety of interests
- To avoid routine
- People contact
- To move quickly
- To be involved in multiple projects
- To make people happy
- To enjoy their work
- To have many different experiences
- Satisfaction
- Innovation

## Top Coaching Tips for SEVENS

- Coach them towards solutions that allow them to maintain variety in their actions.
- Encourage them to be grateful for what they have and where they are right now. Remind them of how far they have come.
- Encourage them to focus on the work in hand as **SEVENS** can often have a very short attention span and easily distract themselves.
- They require a regular burst of 60 seconds coaching throughout the day, every day.
- Coach and think fast with a **SEVEN**
- When formulating an action plan – goals, actions and deadlines must be absolutely crystal clear.
- Refer to the overall vision either for them personally or the team – they love looking at the big picture.•

## THE LEADER
## CASE STUDY

Paul is Managing Director of an 'IT' Company

"On a bad day, whoever is coaching me has to be a brave man!"

"I have strong visions and know exactly what I want. Probably the best way to get me to open up to you is to be direct, and forthright in your approach. I love a challenge and will do whatever it takes providing I agree with the direction in which we are headed."

"I am learning to listen more and show compassion towards others when the going gets rough. I used to explode in front of people but am learning to control this anger more and more."

"It takes a lot for me to show my vulnerable side to people but I have to admit that when I have had great coaching in the past it has been good for me."

"If you break your promises with me I feel let down. By the way it's ok for me to break the rules when it suits me. This is something you are better off accepting if you want to coach me effectively."

"I know I am good at what I do but it is nice to hear it from others. Respect has always been important to me – I was brought up to always show respect for seniors."

## What EIGHTS want

- To be in charge
- To take action
- To be able to rally others to meet deadlines
- To make quick decisions
- To complete everything they start
- To be challenged
- To convince people to do things their way
- Power and authority

## Top Coaching Tips for EIGHTS

- Always admit it if you make a mistake and then move on.
- Leave them alone when they want to be alone.
- Never tell them what they can't do.
- Always keep your promises and appointments with them.
- Be crystal clear when goal setting and make sure you challenge them
- Hold your ground if they become aggressive, and match their energy – get angry with them – not at them.

## THE PEACEMAKER
## CASE STUDY

Joanne is a Group Manager working in a pharmaceutical company

"Coaching is good for me although I sometimes find it difficult to admit I need help and ask for it. I sometime feel pressured if the coach does not allow me to take my time as I prefer to take things more slowly than others in the office."

"Sometimes when I am told to complete actions that I do not want to do I say 'yes' and then do my own thing anyway. I would rather do nothing than voice my objection; or if I feel too much pressure I can sometimes shut down or 'zone out'."

"I like connecting with people and actually like my ideas to be heard but I will not open up unless I feel comfortable in doing so, and know that what I say will not upset people. When I am in meetings I usually have the right answer to discussion points but am often afraid to say anything."

"It's always best if things are put in writing as I sometimes forget what I have committed to. Encourage me to bring deadlines forward or help me finish before the due date works well for me too, because I can sometimes cause myself unnecessary pressure by leaving things until the last minute."

"If you show anger towards me I may well shut down for a long period of time."

"It's nice to feel appreciated and this is probably one of the things that motivates me the most. I like feeling valued and when people give me their undivided attention it can go along way towards my performance. When I am at my best I enjoy working to goals and can be very focused and determined to get things done."

## What NINES want

- To make themselves and others feel at ease
- People to get along with each other
- To negotiate to reach solutions
- To follow agreements
- To stay calm and collected
- To get along with everyone
- To consider the facts patiently
- Harmony
- Routine

## Top Coaching Tips for NINES

- Establish crystal clear goals and deadlines
- Get them to write down their goals and action plans wherever possible – get them to confirm their actions to you in writing
- Always make sure they are 150% committed to the action plan
- **NINES** analyse things when they feel uncomfortable and a slightly faster approach, as with the **SIXES**, gives them less time to think and more opportunity to use their intuition
- Agree to bring deadlines forward – **NINES** have a tendency to leave things to the last minute.
- Use gentle reminders to review their progress.
- Use the re-evaluate step a little more often than with other types.

## Motivate Coaching Tools

There are a wide variety of different techniques you can use to develop infinite flexibility in your approach to motivating your coachees. It is important that the people you coach on a regular basis do not anticipate your approach.

With an awareness of natural motivational styles based on the Enneagram, you can now begin use the following strategies to develop an increasingly flexible approach towards your coaching.

These motivational strategies work well only if you are operating with good intentions towards the people you are coaching. If you don't genuinely care about a person, their success and happiness, then your coaching could well be a waste of time

It is when you truly care and pay attention to what others want, that they achieve their goals, and your natural ability to motivate will soar.  Coaching from the heart is what will motivate your coachees, because they know instinctively that you are committed to their progress

## Changing what Things mean to People

This is known as 'reframing'. In other words, you can change how someone feels about something by changing its context, or frame of reference such that it creates a different and positive meaning.

It is in effect allowing them a genuine, positive perspective, where the benefits outweigh the arguments. The new meaning is naturally more compelling than the old one because the new meaning has more value to the individual.

Reframing works only if the body is fully associated to the new meaning and the subconscious mind has fully accepted the new perspectives as being of more value to them than the old one - anything else is just positive thinking.

This tool is one of the most fun and easiest to use when coaching.

*Example:*

"Coaching takes too much time. It's much quicker to tell someone what to do."

This statement could be rephrased as :

"Have you thought about how coaching could actually save you time?"

Changing the original frame of reference from **taking time** to **saving time** creates a different focus and sensation within the body and mind. The result is that the coachee is naturally empowered to move further forward towards the desired goal.


## PROOF EXERCISE

Make a list of five things that make you feel a little unhappy. Now, offer yourself three different, positive perspectives for each one.

Make sure these are *genuinely* feel-good perspectives, coming from your heart and not your head!


### Story-telling

The use of metaphor helps people to remember large amounts of information and to also make internal thought and emotional shifts that inspire them to change in behaviour.

Television has this powerful effect on us all the time without the viewer even being aware of it. When we find ourselves relating to a particular character and their circumstances in a television series, we may make different decisions as a result of our subconscious mind being influenced by their behaviour and the story line.

What decisions have you made that were inspired by a television programme?

When coaching, questions may not always succeed in motivating people. If this is the case, instead of coaching them directly i.e. going through the front door, it is possible to fool their subconscious mind by using the back door instead, using story-telling techniques

We can use this to our advantage, because the subconscious mind forms parallels with the stories you tell, focusing them in the direction they want to go.

I have the pleasure of working with two people who excel at this. Their training and coaching sessions are highly entertaining and a delight to attend. By the end of the programme it really does not feel like training or coaching at all. Their technique is so subtle that participants often do not even realise that they have been coached!

During training events we use stories that everyone feels good about, relating to Christmas and holidays, but when working one-to-one we make the stories more personal, depending on how well we know the coachee.

A friend of mine, Sarah, who is passionate about horses, was having difficulty in relaxing when practicing the presentation skills that I was teaching her.

We were chatting over lunch and, at the right moment, I told her about another friend who owns a horse, and the time I have been spending with her, using relaxation techniques to quieten her mind and improve her emotional intelligence.

She found that by completely relaxing she has more control. In fact, now she only has to think about what she wants and the horse knows exactly what to do, without her having to make any effort.

It took me less than one minute to tell Nora that story and the results were instantaneous. During the afternoon session she relaxed more into what she was doing and delivered a presentation that appeared more confident and effortless.

**Keys to success:**

- Know exactly what behaviour needs to change i.e. know your outcome
- Find out what the person is most passionate about and use a metaphor or story around that subject – this way they will naturally be more open to listening to you
- Plan your story or metaphor carefully to contain just the right ingredients i.e. the metaphor must contain story lines that demonstrate parallels with the current issues, behaviour you want to change and the positive results.
- Tell them the story when they are relaxed and least expect it

**Motivating a Person using past Experiences**

When a coachee has references of being successful in the past, then it makes sense to tap into those resources again.

Losing weight once and then piling on the pounds again can be upsetting for people. Remembering a time when they felt great about healthy eating and losing weight recovers those motivating feelings and is very easy to do.

Placing themselves back in time, to when they were their natural size and shape, will cancel out their feelings of being overweight and over-eating. So by re-associating with those feelings throughout the day, they will maintain their focus and drive.

These are some of the questions that help coachees motivate themselves:

What did it feel like to be that weight?
Could you allow yourself to remember what it feels like be your ideal weight?
How does it feel right now to know you can regain that ideal weight?
How would it feel right now to have that ideal shape once more?

When a person does not have a past experience that they can refer to, ask them to think of someone they know who is as fit and healthy as they would like to be. Then ask what it would feel like to be that person.

**Summary for Motivate**

**Three most important Things to remember:**

1.  It is all about emotion not logic! Make sure they speak
from their heart and not their heads!

2.  What motivates you may be very different to what
motivates them. Knowing their Enneagram type, use their
core motivations to phrase questions which
create maximum impact in seconds!

3.  Use these tools to increase self-motivation and use
this energy to be in a positive emotional state so that
it rubs off onto your coachee.

# Chapter Ten

Formulate
Generating creative and highly workable Solutions to
achieve Results

**Strategic Thinking**

"This is concerned with the choice of the most appropriate steps out of a
multitude of possible steps. The search is not for a definite solution but for a
policy of behaviour that is more effective than others."

**Edward De Bono**

When your coachee knows what he/she wants and is sufficiently
motivated, then the next step is to brainstorm the actions most

likely to obtain the desired result, in the most effective and enjoyable way.

Have you ever taken some action and then later realised there would have been a much quicker and smarter way to get the same result, had you only taken a couple of moments to think about it beforehand?

It takes a few seconds to allow the coachee to bring to the forefront of their mind *their own ideas* of how they could approach the task. Have them consider the options available to them by using a variety of fast and effective creative thinking tools that help the coachee produce results with the least amount of effort.

Use simple questions such as:

What action will you need to take?
How could you achieve this?
What is the very first step you need to take?

Remember, the solution must be theirs and not yours. Allowing them to take ownership of the solutions encourages them to also think creatively when you are not around. This is a vital building block for self-esteem.

How often do people make fun of other's suggestions and give them a sense that their ideas are not worth listening to?

It is important that you take each and every one of their ideas as positive because the moment you negate a person's idea you are more likely to block their creative flow, and who knows what their next idea will be? – it could be the one answer they are looking for.

After each idea is given, move it to one side and allow enough space for the next positive thought to come through. Step back and consider the array of solutions and have them select the most appropriate having reviewed them all.

Sometimes the level of motivation can drop when a person realises what is involved in achieving their goal.

Watch for any signals that your coachee feels uncomfortable or lacks commitment to any actions. If necessary, begin the **formulate** step again, to uncover an alternative and preferred option.

Also, remember to use the coaching strategies mentioned in the Motivate chapter that highlight the preferred working styles of each Enneagram type and incorporate these strategies into their solutions.

**Uncovering Solutions most likely to succeed**

The quality of your questions can stimulate amazing creativity in your coachees. These questions can be as easy as "what actions are most likely to succeed?"

*Other include:*

- What are the actions/steps you need to now take to achieve (stated objective)?
- What needs to happen next to make progress today with this?
- What do you now need to do?
- What is the smallest step you can take today? (If there is resistance to action)
- What other resources do you have available to assist you with this?
- In an ideal world, what would you do?
- What could you do to make this even easier for yourself to achieve?
- What ideas do you have to improve the results you are getting?
- What could you do to enjoy the process even more?
- What else could you do?
- And if that doesn't work what would you do?
- What have other people in the department done to make it work?
- Who do you know that can help you?
- What support do you need?
- What actions will definitely get you what you want?

Creative thinking should be fun and although it can be a little time-consuming for Results Coaching In 60 Seconds the more specific you are with your questions the faster and better the answers will be from your coachee. Remember, the more you use this coaching system the more people will understand and appreciate the directness and speed of your coaching.

*Here are some examples* :

What three actions will guarantee you achieve this objective?
Which one of these ideas is most likely to work for you?

To save even more time, allow people to go away and think about their ideas and ask them to come back with their plan by a certain deadline. Using this strategy gives them a little breathing space either to come up with the ideas themselves, or to ask other people and then to select the options they feel would work for them.

Always bear in mind that your coachee does indeed have the answers he/she needs. It is just a case of asking the right question which taps into that treasure chest of ideas. However, finding that your coachee is drawing a blank when it comes to generating ideas is not uncommon and can be easily overcome using one of the following strategies.

Never accept the 'I don't know' answer. Why? Because we learn so much more when we discover things for ourselves.

You can respond to "I don't know" in a number of different ways:

- That's ok; if you did know the answer then what would it be?
- What if you did know how to do it?
- In an ideal world, what would you do?
- What would your best guess be?
- What did Sally do in that situation?
- What would Sally do?
- When have you done something similar before? What did you do then?
- Who would know?
- What would you do if you knew you could not fail?

If they are still not responding to you then consider if your coachee has a training need.

## Future pacing

By placing someone into the future, as if they had already been successful and asking them to look back on how they did it, you can often uncover solutions that a person was otherwise unable to access.

Providing you have good rapport with your coachee and they trust you, use the following script to help them to generate ideas. This is wonderful for project planning and working with larger objectives.

"Relax and close your eyes. Now imagine you have achieved this result already, right now. See what you see, hear what you hear and feel how you feel knowing that you have been successful. Now look back over time – and tell me exactly how you did it."

Ask them to tell you exactly what they did and in what order. You may wish to write down their ideas for them.

## Wiping the Slate clean

We often believe that, based on past experiences, an idea will not work and yet how do we know for sure that that is the case? When we can allow a person to delete all moments from their past where they perceived themselves to have failed, then the creative juices can flow more freely and they can make progress.

Clear the mind of your coachee by offering the following brief instruction;

Imagine an altar table in front of you. Dump all your negative thoughts and beliefs onto this table and then wipe the entire contents to the floor. Now, place only positive ideas and solutions back on the table. What do you see?

**Creative Visualisation**


*"When inspiration does not come to me, I go halfway to meet it."*

### Sigmund Freud

By learning to tap deeply into your intuition, a wealth of ideas can be generated quickly and effectively. This method is a tool to tap into a person's intuition. As a coach you will know when they are thinking too hard and when they are just allowing the images to come to them. Conscious mind-chatter is not intuition. If you find this happening, ask them to relax even more and notice what they notice

Relax, close your eyes and imagine sitting in a cinema with a blank, brilliant white screen in front of you. Now, for the next 60 seconds allow images to flash quickly onto the screen holding in mind thoughts and feelings of achieving this objective. Write down whatever your coachee says or even record what they say.

Reflect on the ideas and pictures together and use this as the basis for your action planning. Creative thinking is fun and the more enjoyable and interesting you can make it for your coachees, the better the quality of solutions you will generate.

**If all else fails!**

If all else fails, you can position your own ideas, but only if someone really cannot come up with any of their own. It can be done elegantly and to great effect but should be used as the absolute last resort.

Always ask their permission to give them ideas and only when you have their agreement can you then offer them your solutions. Frame this be saying:

"May I offer you some ideas?"
"Can I make a suggestion?"

Provide them with a minimum of three suggestions, to at least give them a choice of what is more likely to work for them. By providing them with a range of ideas and asking them which one would work best for them, you are still giving them choice and freedom to do what they want to do.

Do not take it personally if they do not think your ideas will work for them. They are entitled to their opinion!

If they are not willing to commit to any action or suggestions, then you know that you have not completed the previous coaching steps well enough so retrace your steps.


**Words that stimulate Creativity**

We know by now that our own language patterns as coaches determine not only how we feel but also how our coachees feel. This means we can use particular words that will stimulate creativity in ourselves and others.

The quality of your questions will determine the quality of ideas you elicit from your coachee. A well-worded question will elicit the perfect answer in the shortest amount of time. There are infinite questions available to you and below are some of the key ones that I use.

In order to smoothly integrate coaching into your natural style of leadership, it is advisable to spend some time creating questions of your own.

You can use the following words as triggers and include them when devising questions that you can use when agreeing action plans with your coachees.

| Create | Discover | Resources |
|---|---|---|
| Options | Uncover | Imagine |
| Intuition | Alternatives | Heart |
| Unique | Wise | Plan |
| Different | Opportunity | Future |
| Wonder | Spontaneous | Limitless |
| Possibilities | Reveal | Open-minded |

For example;

What does your intuition tell you would be the best course of action to get you the result you want?
What other great resources do you have available to you?
What do you imagine would be the best thing to do for you?
What does your heart tell you to do?

Compare these questions with the following:

What do you think you should do?
What action must you take in order to achieve this?
What do you need to do?
What must happen to get this done?

Notice when you ask yourself these questions change how you feel inside.

## Back-up Plans

During this step it is wise to decide on a back-up plan so that should the first one not produce the desired results the coaches knows instinctively what else they can do.

Area managers, for example, who are responsible for the performance of a group of retail stores, may only see their managers once a week or even once a fortnight. So, by spending a few extra moments ensuring team members have a number of options available to them means they will automatically revert to plans B or C without you having to do any further coaching.

*Ideal questions for this are:*

- In the unlikely event that this does not work, what will you do to guarantee you get the results that you want?
- What else could you do should this plan not work for you?
- What is your back-up plan?

Not every 60-second coaching interaction will need a back-up plan, but use it wisely for the most important and larger business objectives to guarantee results.

### Summary for Formulate

### Three most important Things to remember:

1. Use this step to discover what actions your coachee wants to take to achieve the result and, to the best of your ability, ensure the ideas are theirs and not yours.

2. Have fun using a variety of creative thinking tools such as visualisation and future pacing.

3. You don't have to be with them when they formulate their plan – they can do this in their own time and you can review it with them to save you time.

## Chapter Eleven

## Demonstrate
How to further increase Self-Esteem and Confidence?

> *"Motivation is what gets you started. Habit is what keeps you going."*
>
> **--Unknown**

We often say we are going to do things and then do not keep our word and often fail to act on our good intentions. We know what we should do, but find ourselves lapsing into old habits that 'in the moment' appear to feel more comfortable. The degree to which we feel compelled to act is the degree to which we know that we will do whatever it takes to produces results.

Guaranteeing coaching success with people may involve conveying a taste of what it would feel like to take the actions necessary to achieve the desired results. That way you and the coachee can anticipate any resistance to taking action and re-condition the mind and body to be 100% certain of good feelings being associated to following through.

David Beckham bends the ball perfectly into the back of the net to score some amazing goals at crucial moments of a soccer match. His secret – he rehearses those shots in his mind, time and time again, from the moment the ball is placed on the ground, right through to the ball hitting the back of the net and to the feelings of triumph and celebration.

Visual mental rehearsal is the process by which a person can see, hear and feel what something is like without actually doing anything physically. The extent to which they are fully associated to the images they create in their mind is the degree to which the body and mind believes those images and feelings to be true.

Through role-plays are we can act out a scenario, or practice taking action before the actual event. In a coaching situation role-plays are invaluable but can make many people feel uncomfortable. Without them, training only serves as information and information alone does not always give people the confidence to use what they know.

When a person experiences the sensations of following through with actions beforehand it increases their confidence and sense of fulfilment. The body associates taking the desired action as being more pleasurable than taking any other course of action. The subconscious mind and body form an alliance to get the job done!

Without this alliance the mind may know what to do, but the body has been so deeply conditioned to behave otherwise that its natural reaction is to do as it has always done before. You have to recondition the behaviour so the course of action required to achieve results becomes the stronger pattern of behaviour.

Your aim in this step is to 'condition' the new behaviour to such an extent that you guarantee that the most effective course of action becomes automatic, creating the natural confidence to follow through.

This Demonstrate step can be used just on its own. If you spot an opportunity whereby the goal has been established, your coachee has the desire to follow through but is just lacking in a little confidence, a few moments visually rehearsing or role-playing what they need to do whilst feeling confident may do just the trick!

The subconscious mind knows only pictures and what you hold in mind may feel as though it is your reality. There fore it is important that you deliver only the images of what you want to happen in your life to your subconscious mind. That way your energy and focus is entirely on taking action towards what you do want and not on what you don't want.

If you focus on more of the negative of any situation then that is what the subconscious mind thinks you want to create and so brings more of that experience into your awareness.

Demonstrate is an important coaching step because it guarantees that the subconscious mind understands fully what positive experiences you and your coachees would like to create.

I once had a client who was preparing for one of the most important presentations of her career. She was so nervous about this event that she kept seeing herself over and over again in her own mind where everything went wrong!

She was playing a video film in her mind and was imagining people asking questions that she could not answer, floundering with every response. She felt nervous to the point where she felt sick and even though she knew her subject very well indeed, the content of her presentation made no sense at all.

All we did was create a new video film for her that she could replay in her mind's eye several times. It would be a presentation where she could choose how perfect and masterful the presentation would be.

Beginning with the moment she walked into the room, introducing herself to the audience, she created a picture of a self-assured, happy and competent businesswoman. Even more importantly, she got herself to a place where she could absolutely feel what it would be like to deliver a first class performance through the entire presentation, from beginning to end.

From the moment she walked up to the podium at the front of the room she could sense she had their complete and full attention. No longer needing to refer to her notes, she would glance briefly at the slides and allow clear, concise content to flow from her. And, most importantly, she really got a strong feeling as to how this was all running perfectly.

Questions were answered effortlessly and on the odd occasion she would offer to come back with further information as required.

Could I have coached this in 60 seconds? Yes, absolutely. By allowing her time on her own to produce and direct her new film and then asking her to come back to me when she had done so, I could have pointed her towards a more resourceful direction instantly.

In this case I worked with her, running this new film over and over and over again in her mind, so she could no longer play the old film.

The presentation was only a week away. She was committed to replay this movie every day on her way to work, whilst sitting on the train - and enjoy the process. The result was one of the best presentations she had ever delivered.

## The importance of ensuring people are relaxed and fully associated to the new film

This is where we come right back to the importance of being in the heart and not being in the head. To succeed, a person should feel as though they are right there in that moment, transparently feeling great about what they are doing, and not analysing the merits or otherwise of the process.

If your relationship with the coachee is open enough then running through these exercises with them will be easy.

If they have had any bad experiences with role-plays or visualisation in the past, or get embarrassed at acting out scenes in front of you, then it becomes your responsibility to do whatever it takes to relax, motivate them and explain to them the real benefits of doing so.

Ways to make your coachee feel relaxed:

- Make them laugh
- Do the role-play yourself and have fun with it
- Be open to making mistakes yourself so they also feel comfortable in doing so
- Explain exactly how this works and the benefits associated with it
- Give examples of famous people, using your story-telling techniques from the previous chapter and selecting a person that would naturally inspire them!

Matching and mirroring body and language patterns will give you an intuitive sense of how a person is feeling, just as mentioned in chapter three. It is important that you can access, to the best of your ability, the emotional state you want your coachee to go into. For example, if they want to feel more confident show them high levels of confidence yourself.

If you match and mirror them, accessing the required emotional state before they do, then they will naturally feel more comfortable and begin to match and mirror your own positive body language and language patterns. This means you can successfully lead them into experiencing the emotional states needed to get a great result.

Keep your attention on your coachee at all times. I have seen many people practice this mirroring technique, where they get into the right state themselves but forget to pay full attention to their coachee and consequently they loose rapport. So keep your focus firmly on how your coachees are feeling and mirror them, adding a touch of positive energy to bring them along with you.

**Tips on what to say when guiding People through a Visualisation Process**

Visualisation and visual mental rehearsal produce an experience of what it would feel like to be successful, without physically having to role-play or act anything out.

So, if you would like to use an approach other than role-playing, then choose visualisation. It allows your coachee to take charge of creating their own future, as if directing a movie in which they themselves play the lead role.

You can use the following suggestions as a guide to take a coachee through a simple visualisation process. Part of this process is taught in NLP to help people to overcome phobias, but for the purposes of Results Coaching in 60 seconds, I suggest you use it to give people an experience of following through with the type of business actions, which can make them feel confident and fulfilled.

Ask your coachee to completely relax and, if they are sitting down, to place both feet firmly on the floor. Their eyes should be kept shut throughout the entire time. Next you want them to imagine they are sitting by themselves in a cinema and ask them to picture the blank, white screen in front of them.

Instruct them to run a movie film, in which they can see an image of themselves taking the actions they need to take. Tell them they will watch themselves achieving the desired outcome with complete confidence and experiencing the emotions that support them in taking this action.

Make sure they have a clear bright picture in front of them and now ask them to describe in detail what they can see, hear and feel throughout the movie

Until now they would have been seeing themselves on the screen. Now, ask them to place themselves into the picture as though they were doing the actions right now. They should tell you how they are feeling, what they can see through their own eyes and what people are saying to them.

By repeating the exact words that they have just been using themselves, help them to become even more emotionally associated with that picture. Encourage them to see, hear and feel even more of what they are experiencing, making the feelings even stronger.

Get them to mentally replay this film several times, until you sense that they have fully integrated the experience.

Finally, ask them to open their eyes and tell you how they now feel about the objectives and the actions they want to take. If necessary, suggest they do that process on their own over and over again to build even more confidence.

Visualisation is something which can be done on your own and the more you do it , the easier and more effective your real-life actions become. There is no end to the number of times this process can be repeated  - in fact the more the better.

## PROOF EXERCISE

Find someone with whom you can practice using this process and each of you do at least five visualisations . Make sure you experience what it feels like to be the coachee as well as the coach.

Once you have practiced together, use this tool on a daily basis to help rehearse any situations or action with which you feel slight discomfort. Play this positive film clip several times.

### Role-plays

A role-play does not have to entail acting out the entire sequence, although this works very well if you have the time. You could simply ask the questions that simulate one event in the future, without the coachee ever suspecting it is a role-play situation.

Questions such as;

"In that situation, if I were the customer and I said this to you, then what would you do or say?"

Taking a person into that situation, 'as if' it were happening right now, is a role-play and perfect for 60 seconds coaching.

**PROOF EXERCISE**

Use the following questions to explore how you would handle the following coaching    situations by it writing down. Then, role-play each scenario with a coaching buddy or someone you trust.

Imagine you notice that you are discussing action plans without clearly agreeing the objective, what would you say to the coachee to re-focus the both of you?

How would you handle a situation where you find yourself becoming emotionally involved with your coachee and it is hindering your ability to refocus both of you?

Let us say your coachee is not being honest with you, what do you say to maintain rapport and get a better result?

What is most likely to trip you up as a coach?

How would you handle that situation more effectively?

What specifically would you say to someone who could not tell you what he or she wanted to achieve?

**The Golden Rule**

It does not matter what they do or say during a role or visualisation process, even if you think their performance is not up to standard yet, always reinforce the positive suggestions and actions of your coachee with words such as 'that's right' 'great' and 'yes'.

Aim to build momentum in a person, rather than knocking them down. So often I observe coaches giving coachees a list of things they perceive they are doing wrong.

Feedback must be vastly positive and <u>genuine</u>. Do not make up nice things for the sake of it. Only use 'real', positive feedback , because you want to increase their self-esteem, not destroy it.

**The Coach's four Feedback Tips**

1. Point out to them at least three things they did, that were genuinely great.

2. Never use the word "but" – it only negates everything you have just said. "This was great but……" How many times have you heard that said to you? As a coach, I suggest you remove the word 'but' from your vocabulary altogether.

3. Ask their permission first before you give feedback. When you have it, offer them one piece of feedback using specific evidence such as "you used the words xxxxxx, what impact did that have on the customer and what would you say next time that would improve the result for you?"

4. Repeat the role-play again and again to completely integrate the improvements. Offer no further feedback until the next coaching session - unless they specifically ask you for it.

## Using hypnotic Language

During this stage of the coaching process it is productive to make direct suggestions to the subconscious mind. Here are some tips on statements and language patterns you can use.

You will see from this table just what impact the positive phrases we use can have on others, and how by practising great language patterns you can accelerate your coaching results.

| | |
|---|---|
| "And now…….." | Brings your coachee to the present moment and erases what they were previously thinking about. |
| "You may find yourself……" E.g. "You may find yourself really enjoy doing this." | Suggests to the subconscious that doing this will produce great feelings and results. |
| "As you….." E.g. As you now notice how good you feel, what are people saying to you? | Leads a question where you can direct the focus of the coachee onto a positive aspect of the visualisation. |
| Linking these two together - "As you do xyz you may find that abc…" E.g. "As you now step up to the front of the room you may notice that you feel even more confident than you ever have done before." | |
| "That's right and….." | Acknowledges that they are doing well and builds their self-esteem. |

## Modelling

In NLP terms, modelling is the observing and replicating of the successful beliefs, actions and behaviours of others. It involves determining the exact sequence of internal representations (meaningful patterns of information we create and store in our minds) and behaviours that enable a person to produce a specific result.

For example, if you wanted to bake the perfect cake then you would probably find a recipe book that gives the exact ingredients and order in which you mix them together.

In the same way this step of the coaching process may be as simple as helping the coachee to identify someone in the organisation, who has the 'recipe' to create the desired outcome.

It can save a tremendous amount of time if the coachee can refer to people who have already succeeded in a particular area.

Your coachee can copy the basic ingredients and then add their own, to create a unique and even more impressive result. I like using questions that encourage them to model other people's success AND maintain their personal sense of identity at the same time. After all, it is about accessing their own natural state, which may be quite different to that of the person whom they perceive as being successful, whilst drawing on other experiences.

Using coaching questions, you can ask the coachee to call up a mental image of the person used as a model. Then raise their awareness as to what they specifically do that brings them success. Alternatively, you can ask them questions that encourage to them find out more information for themselves.

**PROOF EXERCISE**

Use these coaching questions now, to raise your awareness of the resources available that you may not have considered before that will further develop your coaching skills.

"Whom do you know that, in your mind, is a great coach?"

"What specifically do they do that, in your opinion, makes them a great coach?"

"What could you do right now to replicate?"

"How could you add your own personal touch and do this even better than they can?"

**Summary for Demonstrate**

**Three most important Things to remember:**

1. Use role-plays and visualisation to give the coachee the feelings and experience of being successful and further build their confidence.

2. Always make sure that they are <u>feeling</u> the great feelings associated with the positive events and repeat until you are certain this new behaviour is how they will naturally respond in a 'real' situation.

3. Further advance your communication skills by developing hypnotic language patterns to accelerate progress.

# Chapter Twelve

## Re-evaluate
### Effective Strategies, Tools and Systems for monitoring and reviewing Performance

Reviewing performance is crucial in coaching and leads us to the next important element of the coaching process. The key to fast and effective coaching is utilizing systems and strategies that either make the process of tracking performance simple for you or, better still, guarantee that the coachee will regularly monitor and track their own performance

How nice to always be able to trust that a coachee will follow through with every objective and action, but in reality as humans they sometimes do not.

When someone makes a commitment to achieve an objective, the motivation to follow through increases significantly when they <u>know for certain</u> that their coach is likely to follow up and monitor their progress. You are the person who will hold them to account.

This step can represent the difference between a great coach and an outstanding coach. So keep a record of key commitments, schedule your follow-up and follow through with your coaching reviews every time!

As with all coaching this step is about using questioning techniques and not 'telling' your coachee where they are in relation to their objectives.

A phone call, a chance meeting, or even a further scheduled coaching session will help them to maintain focus on the outcome. The fact that, before the agreed deadline, current performance is reviewed and further strategies put in place if necessary could make all the difference between achieving and not achieving the objective.

It takes seconds to ask questions such as:

> Where are you with……?
> How are you getting on with……?
> What results have you got so far?
> How on track are you?
> How far ahead are you with your project on a scale of 0-10?
> (Where 1 is just started and 10 is finished)

Make this part of the coaching process a priority in terms of your coaching style and enjoy the rewards for yourself and others. Here are some ideas as to how you can make it easy to review performance with your coachee.

**The Value of your Coachee taking full Responsibility for reviewing their own Performance**

The only way your coaching is going to have lasting results is if your coachee takes full responsibility for their performance and experience. This means your monitoring and tracking their performance as well.

During my career at the bank I was fortunate enough to work for one of the smartest managers I have ever met.

Our Monday morning meetings would always have the same structure, which ensured that we had all the information necessary to formulate and agree the objectives and activity for the coming week.

This information would include:
> Results to-date
> Details of targets missed AND the reasons why they were not met
> Key focus areas for the coming week
> Strategies and ideas to guarantee success for the coming week.
> Details of our schedule for that week.

One thing was certain; if we did not have this information all prepared before the meeting, then we would be asked why not. Monitoring our own results certainly did the trick in terms of knowing what we needed to do.

The meetings were quick and very focused. We worked as a team and agreed what we all needed to work on. This manager is one of the very few people I know, who could consistently generate ownership and responsibility in us for the performance in our respective areas.

You can agree the structure of your coaching meetings with your coaches before and have them prepared and ready for every coaching session.

## Keeping track of the Objectives as a Coach

Basic monitoring principles can be applied easily to coaching. Just remember, the aim is to empower your coachee to take responsibility for monitoring their own performance.

A small notebook kept with you at all times enables you to jot down reminders of key commitments your coachees are making. I have known some people use a hand-held tape recorder as well.

Write down the name of the coachee, objective and the date when you would like to re-evaluate their progress. Review this book on a daily basis to remind yourself of the contacts you want to make for that day. A one-minute phone call or a simple re-evaluate coaching question delivered with genuine interest can make all the difference!

By asking your coachees to let you know on a regular basis what their successes have been and what their focus will be for the near future, ensures they keep track of their own performance and make the necessary adjustments.

At the end of a training session I always request that people email me, by a given date, details of what they have applied and the successes they have had in using what they have learned. It is amazing how this simple technique maintains the focus on using what they have learned, even long after the event. In turn it only takes me a few moments to email my personal 'well-done' responses or call and congratulate them in person.

Voicemail messages, faxes and emails are all methods by which people can communicate their progress. You can then review these communications on a daily basis and reply personally to the ones you choose.

A 60 second phone call, fax, email or a voicemail message in return, acknowledging great performance and adding appropriate coaching questions, allow you to utilize your skills consistently, even if you are not always able to meet face-to-face.

## Three golden Questions for reviewing Performance

When practicing this principle during coach training programmes, we find participants often make the mistake of devising their own version of this model, rather than sticking with these three questions - in this order.

Just ask these three questions and wait for the answers. It takes less than 60 seconds. They can be all you need to review progress and performance quickly and effectively. Not only that but you are raising the person's self-awareness all of the time.

1. What went really well for you?
2. What did you learn? (This question presupposes that mistakes are all lessons)
3. What will you do differently next time?

When you have mastered the three golden questions, then you can increase your flexibility by creating positive questions that effectively review performance.

Here are some further suggestions to help you review performance:

- What were your successes in getting to where you are right now?
- When you look back, what good things have you learned?
- How will you apply what you have learned across other areas?

- What have you learned about yourself?
- What impact are these results going to have on your future?
- If someone else were to take on this goal now, what advice would you give him or her?
- On reflection, what could you have done to make this even easier for yourself?
- What smaller objectives did you achieve?
- What improvements have you made?
- Where would you like to see this going now?
- What decisions do you now need to make to improve these results further?
- What level of commitment do you now feel towards this goal?

**Using 'The Wheel' to review Performance across a range of Objectives simultaneously**

This exercise gives an immediate and full picture of how balanced or unbalanced performance is.

We have already used the relationship wheel to assess the quality of our coaching relationships. In exactly the same way we can use it to quickly assess our progress across a number of business areas or personal areas of life such as financial, health etc, simultaneously.

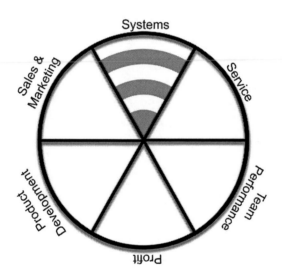

Draw a new blank wheel and divide it into segments, each one being allocated to an area of business performance. Draw lines in each segment to represent the level of performance in each allocated area.

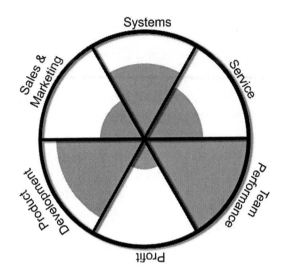

## Tips for reviewing Underperformance

A manager once asked me why all his efforts to motivate his team were not working. He spoke to his key team leaders on a daily basis, agreed objectives and formulated plans brilliantly. I offered to spend time with him because he could not see what else he could do to improve.

His only challenge was that after making people feel great about the progress they had made and ensuring they had a new objective to work towards, he would generally end each meeting by pulling them up on their weak points.

You can imagine how the coachees felt and what was said to other team members when he left the room! All that great coaching for nothing, just because his last point of focus had actually made his coachees feel worse than before!

Your aim is to get the coachees to tell you how they managed in terms of the objective and, if necessary, admit to themselves the <u>real</u> reasons why it did not happen for them. Self-analysis is crucial for improvement.

Give others a safe forum to tell you the truth, without fear of retribution. And in turn allow the coachees to give themselves their own feedback - it will have a much greater impact. Only ever give your feedback with their full permission.

If you meet with resistance, you will need to rely on the strength of your relationship to persist with your coaching. I suggest using the meta-model questions given in Chapter Five to help you uncover the truth.

You want them to bounce back as quickly as possible and refocus on either achieving that objective or moving onto the next. Remember, the moment you judge their performance you lose the power to turn the situation around. Give them five positive comments for every negative one, to ensure the balance is tipped greatly in favour of the good things coming from this experience.

Those who are quickest to judge are often those in possession of the fewest facts. In your genuine desire for the coachee to succeed, it is so easy to fall into the trap of making judgments if you feel your coachee has not given 100%. Just remember, though, that making a judgment takes you further from your natural state and indicates that you have become attached to the outcome yourself.

A friend of mine told me that he was disappointed in his performance the previous week. He had not been as focused as he should have been. I asked what specifically he had not felt focused on, because to my mind I saw his week as being very productive indeed.

His passion was financial trading and he had not achieved the results he wanted, as there had been so many other things that needed to be done that week. Seeing how really down he was, I asked him to remind himself of all his successes in the past week, making sure they outweighed his one disappointment.

I then asked him what he would do differently, if he knew in advance that a similar week's activity would happen again.

"I would schedule my lunch breaks so that they coincide with the time I check my trading information, between 1.30 - 2.30pm. That would give me the time that I need to focus on trading, for better results."

Here are some useful beliefs to hold in mind when using this coaching step. They will support you and your coaching when reviewing what the coachee perceives as underperformance.

> Mistakes come from doing, but so does success.
> Use the mistakes of the past to celebrate greater success in the future.
> Failure is just feedback that you need to change your approach
> Persistence is stronger than failure
> Adversity makes us better people.
> The past does not equal the future.

**Summary for Re-evaluate**
**Three most important Things to remember:**

1. Always review your coachees' performance on a regular basis and when you say you will be in touch with them - keep your promise.

2. Allow them to give themselves the feedback - never do it for them. Only ever give them feedback with their full permission.

3. Always end your re-evaluate stage on a high point, giving at least five positive comments for every negative one

# Chapter Thirteen

## Celebrate
## Effective Recognition Strategies that further increase
## Momentum in Performance

## Knowing how People prefer to be congratulated and praised

Celebrate is about allowing people around you to <u>regularly</u> enjoy feeling successful which naturally compels them to continue to do even more. Knowing beyond a shadow of doubt that we have been successful is one of the ways we naturally increase our self-esteem.

Every great coach knows that a "well done," or even just a smile goes a long way in reinforcing great performance and sustaining levels of motivation. This is the final step that completes the coaching process.

This is the ideal opportunity to allow your coachees to talk about their successes. By doing so you can use your coaching skills to help them remind themselves of what specifically went well for them and indeed what they will use again to further improve their performance.

So often we forget the little things that made the biggest difference to results. Do you allow people to tell you about those little things on a regular basis to reinforce positive feelings? Do you allow them to share their successes with others to integrate these good habits into their everyday behaviour?

As a coach you are, in fact, wiring your coachee's nervous system to associate focusing on specific objectives with good feelings and reinforcing them.

Sincere words of praise are the key to this step but insincere gestures of "Well done" may do more harm than good. You know when a person is genuinely pleased and excited for you when something has gone well so never give praise unless you really mean it.

It is important to understand that people like to be congratulated in one of two different ways.  Those who are **'externally referenced'** respond well to praise given to them by others, whereas the **'internally referenced'** know within themselves when they have done a great job!

These two types of reference can be related to the Enneagram types in a generalised way as follows:

| | |
|---|---|
| The Perfectionist | Internal |
| The Carer | External |
| The Achiever | External |
| The Artist | External |
| The Thinker | Internal |
| The Loyalist | External |
| The Adventurer | External |
| The Leader | Internal |
| The Peacemaker | External |

For types who are externally referenced, then full acknowledgement and praise from you, as a coach will work well.

Internally referenced people, however, prefer to be asked how they feel about what they have achieved.

Questions such as these are ideal for internally referenced people:

"How do you feel now you know this is done?"
"When did you know that you had achieved it?"

Take the time to get know your coachees internal or external frames of reference. Make a list of the people you coach regularly, split into two columns, based on whether you have identified them as having either internal or external. It will make is easier for you to make sure you acknowledge performance in line with their natural style..

**Top Ten Strategies for celebrating Success**

1.    Whenever possible congratulate people face-to-face. A personal visit beats a written memo every time.

2.    Handwritten notes can be very personal. Mary Kay Ashe, one of America's most successful business women would handwrite personal notes and birthday cards to her team on unique writing paper.

3.    Ask someone else to mention to them how well you have said they are doing. Third party positive feedback is even more believable and feels wonderful, because it means people are saying great things about you.

4.    Ask for feedback from the people your coachees work with on a daily basis and be the one to feed it back to your coachees - you become the third party.

5.    Give them a small gift, something they can keep with them, to act as a reminder of their success and thus reinforces the great feelings associated with it.

6.    Make their successes known to someone who is respected in their field and ask them to acknowledge your coachee in writing or even in person. Someone of perceived authority can have an even greater impact.

7.    Use team meetings to praise people in front of other supportive colleagues. This works best for those people who are more externally referenced.

8.    Encourage your coachees to keep a journal and keep a record yourself of peoples' successes, so you can reflect on them. It is all too easy to forget how well we have done in the past.

9.    Build self-esteem by getting them to acknowledge themselves. It strengthens their internal references for the future if you are not on hand to do it for them. A great coach will inspire their coachees to motivate themselves on a regular basis.

10.    Your role in their success can be acknowledged also, so remember to be aware and journal your own successes. Write down any feedback you get from coachees that reflect what a great job you are doing. This will also strengthen your internal frame of reference if you are more naturally externally referenced.

**Focus on the next Objective**

It is amazing how quickly people forget the good stuff around them.

Momentum in coaching is always giving people something new to aim for and as soon as the current objective is achieved, be sure to agree the next goal immediately or as soon as you can thereafter. The resulting **'stacking effect'** on their motivation gives you, as the coach, something upon which to build rather than having to start over again the following week, when the intensity of this positive feeling has died down.

*"Motivation is like food for the brain. You cannot get enough in one sitting. It needs continual and regular top-ups".*

--Peter Davies

**Summary for Celebrate**

**Three most important Things to remember:**

1. Know whether individuals in your team are internally or externally referenced and use the right approach to congratulate them on their performance.

2. Be sincere with your recognition

3. Focus them on the next objective quickly to maintain momentum.

> *"The truth is incontrovertible, malice may attack it, ignorance may deride it;*
> *but in the end there it is."*
>
> **Sir Winston Churchill**

## Integrity and coaching

Integrity has nothing to do with wealth, knowledge, or position and in coaching it is merely about being able to consistently demonstrate honesty and compassion, throughout the entire coaching interaction.

A lack of integrity will sap the energy required to sustain high levels of motivation in yourself and the people you are coaching. Every time you breach integrity your mood changes and you move further away from your natural state and even the smallest of mistakes can linger over you for the rest of the day. Sigmund Freud once said 'Lies make you sick'.

The downfall begins with justification and rationalisation.

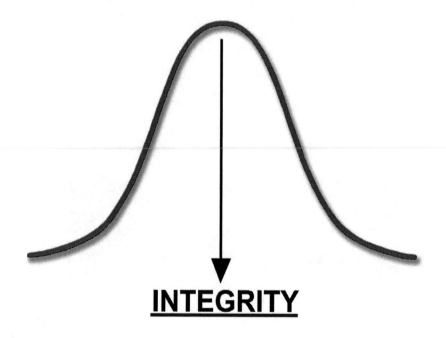

## <u>INTEGRITY</u>

Responsibility is about having the ability to respond and you can only do this if you are relaxed and open with yourself and others.

The more emotional and defensive we become, the harder it is to be honest with ourselves and other people. We are further away from our natural state and in that moment we become drained of energy, leaving us with a much-reduced "ability to respond."

Bill Clinton was, and still is to many people, considered a man of integrity. His emotional defenses, however, were triggered when confronted and he said, "I did not have a sexual relationship with that woman."

As a coach you need to be able to notice the warning signs that indicate you are about to be in breach of integrity and stop yourself before it happens. We call situations like this 'moments of truth'.

## Four Steps to handle an Integrity Problem

1.      Face the problem directly - you can only resolve those problems you are willing to first admit to.
2.      Fully accept the situation - this is just a decision and you can choose in any moment to accept whatever is going on around you. Rationalisation will only send you further away from your natural state and being able using your emotional intelligence. Stop defending yourself and rationalising. Do not ignore the issues and make excuses.
3.      Make a choice - decide what to do and, if necessary give yourself time to make that decision.  Ideally when you know that you are in a higher emotional frame.
4.      In the light of the points made in (3), take action as soon as you can. Procrastination may lead to further rationalisation - create momentum for yourself and just do whatever is necessary.

## PROOF EXERCISE

Think of a situation you have been avoiding and use these four steps to make progress in improving that situation for yourself.

The more you practice this process, the quicker and easier it becomes. You will find yourself accepting more of what is happening around you; you will be letting go of emotional resistance so as to ground yourself; you will be making better decisions 'in the moment' and taking immediate action.

**Are you being authentic with yourself?**

We have all received internal signals that say "don't do this." And then we go ahead and do it anyway, even though it feels uncomfortable. It is all part of being human.

At the same time, the more you relax and accept these internal signals then the more you will maintain your integrity. It may take many lessons to get this right but having a totally honest relationship with yourself is a great start to being able to maintain high levels of integrity with others.


**Are you being authentic with others?**

It is much easier to remember the truth, than remember what lies you have told to people.

One person's stand for integrity has a ripple effect throughout the entire team and if this integrity comes from you, your coachees will move towards it too. It feels good to be in integrity and therefore will naturally improve your performance as a coach.

The following excerpt is taken from **The Corporate Mystic** by Gay Hendricks and Kate Ludeman (Bantam Books).

"I feel activation in my body that is relaxed and alert. I feel curious and very calm. My intuition is heightened. I can make leaps and see images more clearly. I listen better because I am not listening through a filter of 'Are you going to get me?' I feel happy for no reason when I am in integrity."

This energy will transfer to your coachee. If you want to simplify your coaching, then just apply the integrity rule and notice how much more quickly people respond to you, even over a short space of time.

## Are you doing the things you said you would do?

How often do you break agreements with people?

Small agreements, big agreements, it is not a matter of size and there is only one thing to do when you break an agreement, and that is stand up and face it.

## Three Top Tips for managing your Integrity

Here are some suggestions to help you manage your integrity when coaching.

1.      Only make agreements you know you can keep. Not making an agreement with your coachees will be much easier than making one and having to break it later.
2.      Listen to your heart, as it always tells you the right things to do. Make only the agreements you feel heartfelt to keep and not the ones that in your mind will keep you out of trouble. The ones you make in passing that you are not 100% committed to will come back to haunt you later.
3.      If you are in a position where you are making numerous agreements throughout the day, then keep a permanent record of them. You may need to prove the agreement later with someone who was unsure about what they agreed to.

## Communicating with integrity

The truth may sometimes hurt, but it will always help.

Here are some principles that allow us to manage these situations effectively.

This mini-system is great to use with people where you sense they are not being honest with you or themselves.

The art of using it well is to give your coachee the freedom to make mistakes and be willing to forgive them. Cultivate the wisdom to know that others may be right.

Stage One
"I understand………"
"I accept/realize………"
(Shows you hear and understand)

Stage Two
"However I feel……………"
"I have a problem with…………"
(Shows how it makes you feel)

Stage Three
"Therefore I suggest…….."
"I would like to discuss…………"
"I could manage/the alternatives are……………"
(Say what you would like to happen)


## The "Downside" of integrity

Showing your integrity can make a person feel either very safe or, on the other hand, very nervous of you.

For example, a while back I had a potentially very lucrative proposition to make to a local business. The proposal had been very carefully thought through and I felt I had every angle covered. The proprietor saw herself as someone who was a great businesswoman and comfortable in her own environment, but no matter what I did or said, it was as though my confidence threatened her.

Your own confidence and input is not always sufficient. It all depends on the other party's level of self-confidence. The more comfortable you become in being open and honest then the more you begin to know when people are being open and honest with you.

Be sure to meet them where they are as individuals and remember it is part of your role to ensure your coachee is comfortable with you. Only then can you be as honest as you want to be, using the techniques already described.

Never forget that honesty without rapport can be damaging, so be quite certain that your relationships are strong enough to weather the mini-storms.

**Summary for Integrity**

**Three most important Things to remember:**

1. Make integrity agreements with yourself on a daily basis.

2. Watch out for your potential downfall, which begins with justification and rationalisation - develop your emotional intelligence to maintain your natural state at all times

3. Tell the truth and journal your results. By paying attention to the benefits you gain from telling the truth, you will find it easier to use it more often for even greater success.

# Chapter Fifteen

# Case Studies

> *"For the things we have to learn before we can do them,*
> *we learn by doing them."*
>
> **Aristotle**

The following stories provide you with examples of successful Results Coaching in 60 Seconds.

Please note there is an infinite number of ways in which the model can be used successfully. The steps and strategies you choose to use 'in any given moment' are up to you.

To receive the latest free case studies you can sign up to our complimentary newsletter available at www.rc60s.com.

**Situation 1:**

It is the beginning of the working week. Sarah, a District Manager, receives a call from one of her Area Sales Managers, Sam. She can tell that he is unhappy about something.

From previous conversations, Sarah has identified Sam's Enneagram type and knows him to be of a **NINE** (Peacemaker) motivation.

Coaching:

| | | |
|---|---|---|
| Sarah: | "Hi Sam. How was your golfing weekend?" | Relate |
| Sam: | "Not bad thanks. It all went too quickly though." | |
| Sarah: | "What's up Sam? You sound a little down." | |
| Sam: | "I'm ok – just got lots of work on that's all." | |
| Sarah: | "What specifically do you have on at the moment?" | Evaluate |
| Sam: | "I have meetings nearly all week, I have all the performance reviews to do, paperwork, customer complaints and a few other bits and pieces as well." | |
| Sarah: | "What specifically are your two key priorities for the week?" | Stipulate |
| Sam: | "The three performance reviews and catch up completely with my paperwork by Friday." | Clear objective now agreed. |
| Sarah: | "Ok, so on a scale of 1-10, how confident are you that you can finish the reviews and your paperwork by Friday?" | Sarah knows that because he is of a 9 type that she must focus on what he needs to finish. |
| Sam: | "Actually, about 8 out of 10." | |

| Sarah: | "Ok, what is stopping you saying 10 our of 10?" | Evaluate |
|---|---|---|
| Sam: | "Interruptions. My mobile seems to be forever ringing these days." | |
| Sarah: | "Ok, I understand. What do you now need to do to get round that so that you knew you could finish the reviews and the paperwork without being interrupted." | Formulate |
| Sam: | "Well if I turned off the phone for a few hours and worked from home on Tuesday, then that would work." | |
| Sarah: | "Great, so how do you feel now?" | |
| Sam: | "Much better thanks Sarah, sometime I just can't see the wood for the trees!" | |
| Sarah: | "I know what you mean! I will call you tomorrow afternoon to review the performance plans with you."<br>Have a great day, Sam." | To Re-Evaluate next day. |
| Sam: | "Thanks Sarah, you too." | |

## Total Time: 1 minute 5 Seconds

## Follow-up Action:
**Sarah makes a scheduled note to call Sam after 3pm on Tuesday.**

## Situation 2:

Pete is Operations Manager at an exclusive health resort. His Fitness Manager, David (**SIX** type) has been given a stipulated target to recruit 20 new personal training clients over a four-week period, to boost income for the department.

It is now week 2 and only 3 sales have been made in total.

Pete goes to see David in his office.

| | | |
|---|---|---|
| Pete: | "Hi David, I just noticed the sales figures for last week. I see we are a little behind and was wondering what your thoughts were about the sales for this week?" | Relate<br><br>**SIXES** must know that they can trust you. Be honest with them & Evaluate |
| David: | "Yeah, I know we are a bit behind. I just think clients don't want to pay extra for personal training. They are quite happy coming into the gym and doing their own thing." | |
| Pete: | "If that is the case then we may need to rethink the objective. How many clients said that to us last week?" | Evaluate |
| David: | "Well I don't know really, it's just the feedback I am getting from the team." | |
| Pete: | "Right ok, so in your opinion, what do you think the reasons are?" | |
| David: | "I don't think they are talking to people about it." | |
| Pete: | "Ok, what happened last week to make the three sales?" | |

| David: | "Sally made those, she's great and really keen." | |
|---|---|---|
| Pete: | "That's excellent. What needs to happen to encourage more people to sell as a many as Sally?" | Motivate and Formulate |
| David: | "I will have a meeting with them first thing tomorrow morning and ask Sally to share her experiences and ideas and get them working as a team on that." | |
| Pete: | "Great. That's a good idea. Right now, how certain are you that we can change the figures this week?" | |
| David: | "Actually, I am very certain. I have maybe not spoken enough to them about it. That's all." | |
| Pete: | "Would you drop me an email and let me know how the meeting went and if you need any support with this, would you call me tomorrow?" | Re-Evaluate |
| David: | "Yeah, sure." | |

**Time: 1minute 1 Second**

**Follow–up Action:**
**David made a note to speak with David at the meeting on Friday if he had not heard from him before.**

## Situation 3:

Sylvia is a member of a telephone reservations team. She is a great team player (**SIX** type) and works very hard. The supervisor, Jenny, monitors the number of calls waiting by a moving board situated in a prominent position in the room.

When a large number of 'calls waiting' appears on the display board, Jenny notices that Sylvia's response to the client changes from a high standard of service to very mediocre.

Jenny approaches Sylvia about it.

| | | |
|---|---|---|
| Jenny: | "It's been very busy today hasn't it?" | Relate |
| Sylvia: | "Yes, very. I have not had a break all morning." | |
| Jenny: | "I have noticed that people tend to rush the calls when we have a large number of calls waiting which is impacting on service." | |
| Sylvia: | "Well you know what the boss says about getting the calls answered quickly, it does put more pressure on us." | There is a danger here that Jenny could get sidetracked into debating operating principles in the team. Instead she continues to focus on what it is that Sylvia can change – i.e. her own thoughts and behaviour. |
| Jenny: | "What is going through your mind when you know there are so many calls to be answered?" | |
| Sylvia | "This morning I could see the number 8 flashing and I thought, oh no, I have got eight calls waiting." | |

| Jenny: | "Is that true? How many of the calls are actually for you, if you are dealing with someone already?" | Evaluate – By raising Sylvia's awareness she change what the "calls waiting" board means to her personally, and thus she changes her perception, how she feels about it and ultimately how she responds to the information. |
|---|---|---|
| Sylvia: | "Well with 10 of us in the team probably only 1 if that." | |
| Jenny: | "How will knowing that change your behaviour?" | Formulate |
| Sylvia | "I won't be in such a hurry to move onto the next client." | |
| Jenny: | "Great." | |

## Time: 58 seconds

## Follow-up Actions:

Jenny observes Sylvia.
Jenny makes it clear to the team that the purpose of the call waiting board is to highlight to people not on the phone that we have customers waiting.

## Notes:

The thought, "I have 8 calls waiting," was what was driving Sylvia's behaviour subconsciously. By making her aware of this belief and changing what it meant to her Jenny was able to effortlessly change her focus to produce a results that was good for Sylvia, Jenny and the company.

## Situation 4

John is Area Manager for a building society and is making calls mid-week to review the sales progress of his Branch Managers.

His next call is to Julie who is a type **TWO** - the Carer.

| | | |
|---|---|---|
| Julie: | "Hi John" | |
| John: | "Hi Julie, how are you? How are you doing with the sales this week?" | Relate and re-evaluate.<br>**TWOS** like to be called and spoken to. So this in itself is enough to motivate Julie |
| Julie: | "Well, insurance sales are up and we have exceeded target this week. Accounts opened is ok, but we are short of savings plans." | |
| John: | "You have done well with insurance. That's great – no other branch has done that just yet. Just remind me, what exactly are we aiming for this week in terms of savings?" | Stipulate – it's important to refocus the coachee on the specific objective |
| Julie: | "£30,000 in balances by Friday." | |
| John: | "Where are you now?" | Evaluate |
| Julie: | "£12,000 and I can't see how we can make it!" | |
| John: | "When you have hit the target before at the last moment, what exactly did you do?" | Motivate - John is using good experiences from the past to ensure Julie can feel good about this again. |

| Julie: | "Sarah called a couple of clients she knew, who had already told her they were expecting some money in. So she asked them if she could put the monies straight into a savings account and they could then earn interest immediately." | |
|---|---|---|
| John: | "Ok, so what options do you have to make it easy for the team to achieve this target before Friday?" | Formulate |
| Julie: | "I will ask the team whom they know and ask them to make a number of calls." | |
| John: | "That's great. What if they do not have any names – what could your back-up plan be?" | Formulate |
| Julie: | "I will ask the staff on the counter to pay attention to anyone paying in larger cheques – they too have helped us in the past." | |
| John: | "Excellent – well done! Let me know how you are getting on tomorrow by email" | Celebrate – and re-evaluate because John is ensuring that he knows a day before the deadline that Julie will be back on track. |

**Time:** 1 minute 34 seconds

**Follow-up action:**
John makes a note that Julie will email him tomorrow and if he has not heard from her, then he will call her before Friday.

## Situation 5

Mark is a lab technician and operates from an Enneagram type **NINE**.

His Team Leader, Sarah, has agreed with Mark that she will see him at the same time every morning, because she knows that **NINES** prefer routine.

It is Monday morning and Sarah goes to see how Mark is getting on with his latest project.

| | | |
|---|---|---|
| Sarah: | "Hello Mark, how was your weekend?" | Relate |
| Mark: | "Good, thanks." | |
| Sarah: | "What are the project objectives for this week?" | Stipulate<br>**NINES** like routine and so Sarah uses much the same approach every Monday. This makes him feel more relaxed. |
| Mark: | "To register the complete findings of stages 2 and 3 of the experiment." | |
| Sarah: | "Ok, by when exactly?" | Stipulate |
| Mark: | "Wednesday." | |
| Sarah: | "Good, do you think you will make that deadline? | Evaluate |
| Mark: | "I think so." | |
| Sarah: | "On a scale of 1-10 how certain are you?" | Evaluate |
| Mark: | "7" | |
| Sarah: | "What stops you saying a 10?" | Evaluate |
| Mark: | "The equipment has not arrived yet and even though I have chased the order it might not be here in time." | |

Sarah:     "Ok, what else can we do?"

Mark:      "Nothing if the equipment does not arrive."

Sarah:     "I understand. Who is expecting the results?"

Mark:      "David."

Sarah:     "What can you arrange with him to keep the project on track overall?"

Formulate

NINES have a tendency to leave things to the last minute and fall behind, so it's important to agree timescales with them to keep things on track.

Mark:      "I will call him and arrange to do experiments 3 and 4 today

Sarah:     "Good idea, would you email me to let me know that David is ok with that and confirm the adjusted plan and timescales for each experiment?"

Motivate - agreements in writing naturally give NINES more sense of commitment.

Mark:      "Yes, I will."

Sarah:     "That's great – well done – I will see you tomorrow."

## Time: 1 minute 17 seconds

## Follow-up Action:
Sarah knows if she has not received an email from Mark that she can review the situation the following day and makes a note to do so.

## Notes:

As the coach your focus must always be on the overall objective throughout the interaction, so that you can ask questions that move people forward regardless of any obstacles in their way.

**Situation 6:**

Sally is an Enneagram Type 2(Carer) and manages a team of IT consultants who produce software programmes.

Her coachee in this example is Mark who operates from a Type 9 (peacemaker) has been asked to complete a project for a company called CitySpec by Friday.

This is how the entire coaching model using all of the eight steps can be used to coaching quickly and effectively:

Today is Tuesday

| Sally | Using releasing techniques and simple breathing exercises Sally focuses her mind on her coaching interaction with Mark. | Sally pays attention to her thoughts and feelings toward Mark and the project and lets go of any limiting sensations and assumption to ground herself in a space of openness and clear thinking before approaching him. | Natural State |

| Sally | "Hi Mark, how's things?" | Sally knows that Mark is a type nine and therefore dislikes people putting pressure on him. She also knows that she must speak little more slowly and give him her undivided attention.<br><br>She also pays attention to language patterns used by Mark throughout the conversation and matches these patterns wherever possible. | Relate |
| Mark: | "Yeah, not bad, really busy though with this CitySpec project." | | |
| Sally: | "David mentioned we had another project. What exactly is it and when does that need to be finished." | Sally asks Mark to clarify the specific objective. | Stipulate |
| Mark: | "It's an online customer survey with 19 questions that needs to be up and running by Friday." | | |

| Sally: | "Where are we right now with it?" | Where is he now in relation to where he wants to be? | Evaluate |
| --- | --- | --- | --- |
| Mark: | "The basic programme is in place, it's just the input now and that's what takes the time as you know." | | |
| Sally: | "I know. CitySpec called yesterday saying they really appreciated the time you spent with them yesterday and the work you are doing this week." | Peacemakers are externally focused and like to know that others genuinely appreciate their personal efforts. | Motivate |
| Mark: | "Great, I like those guys." | | |
| Sally: | "So, what will be the plan to finish the project this week?" | Sally makes sure that mark has a workable strategy to complete the task on time. | Formulate |
| Mark: | "I will work on this input all day today and tomorrow. Simon has offered some help so I could ask him on Thursday to help me test the system ready for Friday." | | |

| Sally: | "Great. Show me what the testing will involve on Thursday." | Sally ensures that Mark is visualisation and associating himself to completing the project successfully | |
|---|---|---|---|
| | Mark completes a demonstration using a similar system. | | |
| Sally: | "Would you send me an email on Thursday morning to let me know how this is going?" | Sally makes sure mark has the responsibility of keeping Sally updated and himself on track. | Re-Evaluate |
| Mark: | "Yeah sure." | | |
| Sally: | "I will make sure that Bob knows CitySpec like what you are doing. Well done!" | Mark is externally focused. Bob is the Managing Director and Sally knows that this good word will continue to keep Mark more motivated through the week. | Celebrate |
| Mark: | "Thanks." | | |

**Time: 1 min 28 seconds**

**Follow-up Action:**
Sally notes in her diary to follow-up with Mark on Thursday

**Situation 7:**

Michael is Area Sales Manager for electrical component manufacturers.

His sales team of five is widespread throughout the UK.

In this team are three people who operate from an Enneagram type **SIX**, one who operate from a type **THREE** and another who operates from a type **NINE**.

Knowing this, he has devised a strategy to keep his whole team motivated and on track, with less effort than ever before.

The **SIXES** enjoy teamwork and the **NINES** enjoy connecting with people. So, a regular fortnightly group meeting is a must for the team.

The type **THREE** is naturally more self-motivated to achieve sales and so Michael agrees a weekly review only and daily email feedback to monitor his progress.

For the **NINES** and **SIXES** Michael contacts them by phone every day: the **NINE** always first thing in the morning. to agree specific objectives for the day and the **SIXES** throughout the day, to increase levels of responsibility when required and develop team spirit.

All in all, using his Enneagram knowledge, his coaching calls only take him a total of 20 minutes every day, instead of the much lengthier calls he was used to before.

# Chapter Sixteen

# Developing a Results Coaching in 60 Seconds Culture across your Team

> "If people are coming to work excited . . . if they're making mistakes freely and fearlessly . . . if they're having fun . . . if they're concentrating doing things, rather than preparing reports and going to meetings - then somewhere you have leaders."
>
> **--Robert Townsend**

## The Coaching Culture

For me, this chapter is the purpose of this book because a person, who is inadvertently influencing your coachees away from their dreams and goals, rather than towards them, could destroy your great coaching efforts in a heartbeat.

The overall levels of morale can be so low in your team (and by team I mean business colleagues or even family and friends) that you may at times risk being pulled down with them. In meetings and gatherings are the majority of people maybe focusing on what they can't do as opposed to what they can do?

Negative emotions drain us of energy. The balance of these emotions within the team must be heavily tipped towards the positive, to stand the best chance of producing results.

Building highly collaborative and productive teams takes time. Yet with this coaching system you can develop a strong coaching culture that has everyone taking full responsibility, both for their individual and team performance.

What if your team were able to coach each other in less than 60 seconds consistently to produce results?

What if your team became so supportive of each other that the moment one person felt uninspired or was lacking in focus another could inspire and focus them instantly? How would life change for yourself and the people around you?

Clarify what a coaching culture means to you personally. Use your visualisation skills and goals setting techniques to give yourself a crystal clear picture of what it is you want to create within your team. You are then better prepared to select the best exercises from the following training plan or, indeed, formulate your own plan to achieve the results you are looking for in the quickest time. This is where the model for 'Keys to an Achievable Outcome' will help you.

What specifically do you want from your team in terms of coaching?

Where are you now in terms of developing a coaching culture across your team?

What will you see, hear, feel, etc., when you have it?

How will you know when you have it?

What will this great coaching culture achieve for you or allow you to do?

Is it only for you?

Where, when, how, and with whom do you want it?

What do you have now, and what do you need in order to achieve your outcome?

- Have you ever had or done this before?

- Do you know anyone who has?

- Can you act as if you have it now?

- For what purpose do you want this?

- What will you gain or lose if you have it?

- What will happen if you get it?

- What won't happen if you get it?

- What will happen if you don't get it?

- What won't happen if you don't get it?

**Integrating Results Coaching into your Team's natural Behaviour**

A couple of years back I was in a position where I had 32 people in a team. This was simply too many for me to coach effectively on a daily basis and still focus on the needs of the business. So, I selected 8 people in my team who would benefit most from coaching and made sure that I connected with them every single day.

Given tricky management situations such as this, you have to develop the most effective strategy to develop the coaching skills of team members. In my case the solution was to focus the most coaching on the key players and develop their skills to do the same with their key players and so on.

Actually teaching coaching skills is the fastest way of learning to apply the principles. One of my closest friends once commented on how rarely, if ever, I give excuses as to why something cannot be done. The simple fact is that when I am teaching it every day, I cannot help but adopt a positive mindset and focus.

Decide who your key players are within your team and focus your daily coaching activity on them.

This plan shows how you can introduce coaching to the people around you and develop a team committed to the development of their coaching skills and the happiness and performance of the people around them.

Feel free to modify it and tailor it to your own needs and circumstances. It is there to inspire and help you with the first stages of your own strategy. How you deliver each element is entirely up to you.

This is a simplified overview of a template that you can use. For further training material and an abundance of team activities and games for use with coachees to develop these skills, you may wish to consider attending our trainer accreditation programme.

## Step One

Hold your first meeting to do the following:

Introduce the concept of Results Coaching In 60 Seconds.
Agree and commit to team agreements and rules
Agree to practice these rules for the next week, journal their successes and feedback to the team the following week.

## Step Two

Hold your second meeting to do the following:

Feedback your successes and results from the first week
Review and remind each other of the agreements and commitment from the first week
Learn the names of the eight steps in the coaching model
Agree to learn one new element of the model and practice it throughout the day e.g. SMART objectives
Agree a method by which you can communicate these lessons to each other (fax, email or phone.)

See the next section of this chapter for ideas on how to do this. You may wish to change your approach every week to make it more interesting.
Continue to journal your successes and review them at meetings on a weekly/monthly basis.

## Step Three

Continue with the regular meetings until all of the basic coaching principles have been integrated and use the questionnaire from Chapter One to review the progress of individuals on a regular basis.

## Step Four

Hold a meeting to do the following:

Introduce the Enneagram and identify the types within the team. Agree to read and learn about their own coaching type, their strengths and weaknesses.
Continue to journal successes and review

## Step Five

Hold a meeting to do the following:

Practice identifying the types of other members of the team and coaching each other in line with your Enneagram type.
Use the following questionnaire and self-coaching tool to assess and review progress.
Continue to journal successes and review

## Full Evaluation Questionnaire

The following questionnaire has been designed to provide a benchmark.

Use it to identify and further develop aspects of your own coaching skills and those of coachees, taking the Enneagram and the Results Coaching in 60 Seconds Model.

It is all too easy to forget what progress we have made with our skills levels.
So I would encourage you to assess current status and then reassess them regularly, as an important motivator for continued growth.

Use the following matrix to measure yourself in terms of coaching skills and repeat the questionnaire regularly to measure your improvement.

4 - always
3 - frequently
2 - occasionally
1 - never

| Your Natural State | | | | |
|---|---|---|---|---|
| I am always completely relaxed in my approach to coaching. | 1 | 2 | 3 | 4 |
| I am always operating from the healthy aspects of my Enneagram type. | 1 | 2 | 3 | 4 |

**Core Beliefs of a Coach**
Your beliefs determine your behaviour as a coach. Get a sense of how strong your beliefs are and if you have difficulty in believing one or two of them then act as if you do all the same for a few days and notice the results.

| | | | | |
|---|---|---|---|---|
| I believe all people have unlimited potential and have the ability to achieve results. | 1 | 2 | 3 | 4 |
| I believe people do the very best they can with the emotional and physical resources they have available to them. | 1 | 2 | 3 | 4 |
| I believe we all have the ability to change. | 1 | 2 | 3 | 4 |
| I believe that people are not their behaviour and that if I fully accept them as a person I can support them more effectively in changing their behaviour. | 1 | 2 | 3 | 4 |
| I believe that coaching must be aimed at improving a person's entire experience. | 1 | 2 | 3 | 4 |
| I believe that there is no such thing as failure, only feedback. | 1 | 2 | 3 | 4 |

| | | | | |
|---|---|---|---|---|
| I believe if I am not getting the appropriate response from a person that it is my responsibility to change they way I am communicating with them. | 1 | 2 | 3 | 4 |
| I believe that coaching can be highly effective in 60 seconds. | 1 | 2 | 3 | 4 |
| I believe that often the biggest changes can be made from making the slightest of adjustments in behaviour. | 1 | 2 | 3 | 4 |
| I believe coaching is about allowing people to discover answers for themselves. | 1 | 2 | 3 | 4 |
| I always ask permission before making suggestions. | 1 | 2 | 3 | 4 |
| I never give advice. | 1 | 2 | 3 | 4 |

| **Objective Setting** | | | | |
|---|---|---|---|---|
| I always have a clear objective in mind with every coaching session I do. | 1 | 2 | 3 | 4 |
| I always request that the person I am coaching clarify their specific goal in their own words. | 1 | 2 | 3 | 4 |
| I always know if the person I am coaching truly believes that the goal is achievable. | 1 | 2 | 3 | 4 |
| I always make sure that every goal agreed has a timescale. | 1 | 2 | 3 | 4 |

| | | | | |
|---|---|---|---|---|
| I always make sure that objectives are measurable. | 1 | 2 | 3 | 4 |
| I always know make sure that the goals are in the best interest of everyone concerned, including the coachee and the business. | 1 | 2 | 3 | 4 |

| **Relate** | | | | |
|---|---|---|---|---|
| I always take full responsibility for building and maintaining rapport with the people I am coaching. | 1 | 2 | 3 | 4 |
| I prefer to listen rather than do the talking. | 1 | 2 | 3 | 4 |
| I am always open to receiving feedback, both positive and negative from my team. | 1 | 2 | 3 | 4 |
| I always align my language patterns to theirs. | 1 | 2 | 3 | 4 |
| I always match an aspect of my physiology to theirs. | 1 | 2 | 3 | 4 |
| I feel confident that I can build and maintain rapport with anyone. | 1 | 2 | 3 | 4 |
| I always summarise and reflect what is being said to ensure full understanding. | 1 | 2 | 3 | 4 |
| I always give people my undivided attention and provide a good working space where we will not be interrupted. | 1 | 2 | 3 | 4 |
| I am happy to coach people considered to be of a higher status to me within the organisation. | 1 | 2 | 3 | 4 |

| | | | | |
|---|---|---|---|---|
| I can show empathy towards people without getting myself caught up in their emotions. | 1 | 2 | 3 | 4 |
| I always ensure at least 80% of my questions are open ended. | 1 | 2 | 3 | 4 |

| **Evaluate** | | | | |
|---|---|---|---|---|
| The people I am coaching always have a very good understanding as to where they are against the agreed objectives. | 1 | 2 | 3 | 4 |
| I am confident in giving constructive and specific feedback. | 1 | 2 | 3 | 4 |

| **Motivate** | | | | |
|---|---|---|---|---|
| I always know what is most important in terms of values of the people I am coaching and can use them elegantly to motivate them to follow through to complete an objective. | 1 | 2 | 3 | 4 |
| I know what the core motivators are for each of the 9 Enneagram types and how to use them. | 1 | 2 | 3 | 4 |
| I always seek to establish what their core issues are and work with them. | 1 | 2 | 3 | 4 |
| I am confident in being able to reframe a person's viewpoint to motivate them | 1 | 2 | 3 | 4 |

| **Formulate** | | | | |
|---|---|---|---|---|
| My coachees always have a clear action plan in their minds as to how to achieve their objective. | 1 | 2 | 3 | 4 |

| | |
|---|---|
| I always ensure people have back-up ideas of how they can achieve their goal if their first plan does not work. | 1  2  3  4 |

| **Demonstrate** | |
|---|---|
| I can use role-plays and visualisation effectively to build a person's confidence and give them an experience before they take necessary action. | 1  2  3  4 |

| **Re-evaluate** | |
|---|---|
| I am proactive in tracking people's performance and always follow up with them after coaching. | 1  2  3  4 |
| I always have the appropriate tracking systems to monitor performance and feedback results. | 1  2  3  4 |

| **Celebrate** | |
|---|---|
| I always congratulate people appropriately for their successes and their efforts. | 1  2  3  4 |
| I can easily identify if a person is internally or externally referenced. | 1  2  3  4 |

Total Score_____

Date_____

Now use the following self-coaching record sheet to take your coaching skills to the next level.

According to the results of your questionnaire, what are your key strengths when using the Enneagram and Results Coaching in 60 Seconds?

What are the two priority areas for you to develop right now?

What are your specific objectives for these areas over the next month?

What will your score be by the end of next month?

What do you want to do and what are you absolutely committed to doing that will ensure this definitely happens for you?

# Five Strategies for managing those who resist Coaching

Why are there so many people who want to build up the weak by tearing down the strong? Why is it that the non-achievers are quick to criticise, question and belittle the achievers?

Having people on your team with such a mindset can be very damaging. They are often resistant to coaching, but not necessarily terminally so. Here are some strategies you may wish to consider using with them to turn them around.

Once you have identified those who are coaching-resistant, if there are a number of them it is a good idea to make sure you do not have them all working together. Their combined energy will make it harder for you to change their perceptions.

Here is what to do:

1. Where possible, get them working with the people most open to coaching, so they are outnumbered and their mindset has no choice but to question their own beliefs about the value of coaching.

2. Disclose pieces of information about yourself that will allow them to see you understand their viewpoint. It is all about rapport. This means finding something of value that you both have in common and that shows you completely understand how they feel. Then, and only then, can you turn the situation around.

3. Create metaphors (see Chapter 8) that highlight the personal consequences to people who close themselves down to coaching.

4. Connect with them socially and uncover their deepest values. Find out what is most important to them and help them achieve a result in an area which is of prime priority

to them. As soon as you get one win, then you will begin to change their mind.

5. Ultimately, as a last resort, you may have to consider removing them from the team. If people are doing more harm than good, then the rest of your team will suffer. I recently met a manager who decided to replace 75% of his team over a period of 18 months because their combined attitude was making it difficult to change mindsets. It is a brave move, but one which over time will reap rewards.

## The four Team Agreements

I am indebted to the author, Don Miguel Ruiz. The following are based on his book 'The Four Agreements', which reveals the source of limiting beliefs.

**Always do your best** – Avoid self-judgement and just do the best you can at every moment.

**Don't take anything personally** – What others say is a projection of their own reality. Be open and at the same time immune to their opinions.

**Be impeccable with your word** – Speak with integrity and with a genuine sense of caring for each other.

**Don't make assumptions** – Use questions to understand fully before jumping to conclusions and be clear with your own communication.

As a team, it is important that you make agreements and stick to them. Ask the team to commit to them in order to support themselves and each other. You can then monitor behaviour more closely and ensure that we are creating a supportive environment, giving everyone much greater chance of success.

## Summary – Developing a Coaching Culture

### Key Points to remember

1. Know what a coaching culture means to you and how you want people in your new team to be, before planning your training activity.

2. In large coaching teams, consider the most important 8 people in your team and focus on the development of their coaching skills. Then focus them on the developing the skills of the people around them.

3. Learn how to handle difficult members of your team who resist being coached and who are damaging to your overall vision

4. Use the Four Agreements to build solid team beliefs

# Chapter Seventeen

Persistence

> *Looking back it seems to me,*
> *All the grief that had to be*
> *Left me when the pain was o'er*
> *Stronger than I was before*
>
> *-unkown*

## Order and Chaos

Commit yourself now to mastering the techniques explained and demonstrated in this book. There are no deadlines and it does not matter how long it takes you. What is important is that, like regular exercise, you do a little every day and watch your coaching muscles build over time.

Abraham Lincoln failed in business twice, lost the woman he loved the most when she died, suffered a nervous breakdown and was defeated in over eight elections before being elected for President of the United States in 1860.

It was Ilya Prigogine, a Nobel Prize Winning chemist who established that:


**'Order emerges not in spite of chaos but because of it'**


Evolution and growth are inevitable. If learning to be a master coach or master of anything for that matter feels overwhelming, then reminding yourself of this quote will help you.

338

Remember learning to read or learning to drive? Seemed complicated at first didn't it? Well, from those first moments of chaos when you had to remember exactly what to do and in what order, your skills evolved into effortless reading– from chaos comes order.

So, however you feel right now about integrating these skills into your natural leadership style, know that from chaos comes order and soon you will be coaching in 60 seconds.

Taking these practices and using them daily is an opportunity to grow as an individual, and become an even stronger coach and manager. Do persist. As a coach you will be supporting people through their "Prigogine moments", as they stretch and expand their personalities and life experience.

Marathon runners experience something called **hitting the wall**. The exhaustion and pain increase to a point where they feel they cannot carry on. Then, suddenly, the resistance bubble inside of them bursts and releases much tension, taking their running to another level.

This is what I call a 'priogine moment', because ultimately the athlete has a choice as to whether or not to keep running or give up the race altogether. One thing is for sure: if they sit down for 15 minutes they are less likely to pick themselves up again and finish the race.

Treat this like a practical training programme that allows you to build great coaching muscles over time.

Doing too much on one day can be dangerous. It is like a weightlifter taking on too much at the bench press machine - one too many lifts may just burn you out for days 2,3 and 4. So my advice is take it easy and really take time to enjoy the journey of becoming an outstanding coach.

At the same time bear in mind, though, that lifting just a couple of pounds will do little to build the coaching muscle and of course doing nothing will not develop it at all, and in fact it may just waste away.

Enjoy the small steps, stretch yourself a little and celebrate the bigger and more consistent victories over time.

The 10 most common reasons why Results Coaching in 60 Seconds does not work for people are:

1. They do not have a specific objective in mind and begin talking about actions before deciding on what they are aiming for.
2. They get wrapped up in people's excuses and feel sorry for their situation, instead of using their questions to positively influence the situation in the moment.
3. The coach analyses the problem for the coachee and gives their opinion on what course of action they should take instead of trusting the coachee to have the answers and using great questions to focus them on achieving the goal.
4. They have no belief that the people they are coaching can get results.
5. They take responsibility away from the coachee by offering to do the activity for them.
6. The coach senses the coachee is uncomfortable and instead of turning them around emotionally and building their confidence, they back away from the objective altogether.
7. They ask too many questions to cover eventualities, taking over 30 minutes to coach a person around one objective.
8. They do not follow up with the coachee.
9. They enjoy the training programmes and reading the material, then do not practice on a daily basis.
10. They make coaching more complicated than it needs to be!

*"Leadership is not so much about technique and methods as it is about opening the heart. Leadership is about inspiration -- of oneself and of others. Great leadership is about human experiences, not processes. Leadership is not a formula or a program, it is a human activity that comes from the heart and considers the hearts of others. It is an attitude, not a routine."*

*--Lance Secretan*

Coaching is a passion for me. I love helping people be who they want to be and have what they want to have. If you would like first hand experience of developing your Results Coaching in 60 Seconds Skills, then my team and I will be delighted to meet you at one of our seminars.

I wish you all the very best with your coaching. Have fun!

Anne Thomas

*Formulate and stamp indelibly on your mind a mental picture of yourself as succeeding. Hold this picture tenaciously. Never permit it to fade. Your mind will seek to develop the picture...Do not build up obstacles in your imagination.*

**- Norman Vincent Peale**

# Bibliography

The Wisdom of the Enneagram by Don Richard Riso and Russ Hudson
Published June 1999 Bantam Books

The 9 Ways Of Working by Michael J Goldberg
Published 1996 Publishers Group West

The Corporate Mystic by Gay Hendricks and Kate Ludeman
Published 1996 Bantam Books

Unlimited Power by Anthony Robbins
Published 1986 Simon and Schuster Ltd

Awaken the Giant Within by Anthony Robbins
Published 1992 Simon and Schuster Ltd

Coaching For Performance by John Whitmore
Published 1992 Nicholas Brealey Publishing Ltd

The Seven Habits of Highly Effective People by Stephen R. Covey
Published 1992 reprint Simon and Schuster Ltd

The Essential Enneagram by David Daniels M.D.
Published 2000 Harper Collins

The Sedona Method© by Hale Dwoskin
Published 2003 Sedona Press

Wooden - A lifetime of Observations And reflections On And Off The
Court by Coach John Wooden and Steve Jamison
Published 1997 Contemporary Books

The Inner Game of Work by Timothy Gallwey
Published 2000 The Orion Publishing Group Ltd

The Four Agreements by Don Miguel Ruiz
Amber Allen Publishing

The Users Manual For the Brain by Bob G. Bodenhamer and Michael
Hall 1999 Crown House Publishing

**"If you find that you learn better from a training programme and like to use a book to back up that learning, then join us for our one-day Open Foundation Seminar."**

*Public and In-Company events NOW available!*

If you would like to receive some of the finest coaching training, develop highly effective skills that save you a great deal of time and learn how to make full use of your natural coaching style, then this seminar is for you!

### Here is a summary of the benefits you receive

✓ **Over 350 business coaching tools and techniques**
Many of these tools will be demonstrated and you will have the opportunity of practising many of them with our team of master trainers.

✓ **One-day intensive training programme**
You and your colleagues can learn the fundamentals of Results Coaching in 60 Seconds in one day and spend less time away from the business.

✓ **Personal Enneagram Profiling**
One of the simplest and most powerful of profiling tools that give you an advantage in any coaching interaction

✓ **Advanced Emotional Intelligence Training**
Expert training on how to handle even the most difficult of coaching situations quickly and effectively

✓ **Coaching Toolkit**
Packed with quick reference guides, templates for coaching records, tracking systems and more

✓ **FREE Follow Up Telephone Seminar *plus* 8-week Email Coaching Programme**
The option to join us for a further 2-hour telephone seminar with the Master Trainers, review the programme, learn even more techniques, share experience and answer any further questions and receive tips and tools everyday to sustain momentum in your coaching development long after the event

✓ **One to One Coaching**
Personal coaching and support from our master trainers throughout the entire programme.

✓ **Guest Speakers**

You will be entertained by one of our many guest speakers, all of who are experts in their field relevant to business coaching

Now, you are probably wondering how and why we can do all those things.
Let me explain.

This one-day programme begins by giving you an overview of the eight step model to Results Coaching in 60 Seconds© and a demonstration of exactly how it works.

You will then learn the tool and techniques required to demonstrate each of the eight steps to a high standard.

You will gain personal insights that give you an understanding of your own thought processes and behaviour patterns that can enhance or detract you ability to coach, enabling you to manage your skills, speed and focus consistently.
Our experienced Trainers will coach you using 'real life' examples so that you can integrate the tools and demonstrate effective Results Coaching in 60 Seconds©.

By the end of the programme you will be able to use basic techniques successfully, over the telephone and face-to-face, to produce results.

And , finally, you will receive email coaching for 330 days following the event to assist you in building momentum from the training event itself and applying Results Coaching in 60 Seconds© techniques every day.

**Regardless of your level of experience, we guarantee to improve the performance of every participant who attends the programme.**


**PROGRAMME OBJECTIVES:**

· The eight steps to effective Results Coaching in 60 Seconds©.
· How to access your most resourceful and most natural coaching state consistently
· How to use highly effective questions to elicit information quickly and raise the awareness of people.
· How to elicit and agree specific objectives within 20 seconds
· Specific strategies to effectively deliver each of the 8 steps

· The nine fundamental motivational types of the Enneagram and why you need to know yours as a coach.
· What are you core motivators as a coach?
· How the conditioned patterns of each type impact the way they communicate with other people.
· How your motivational type affects your performance both as a manager and a coach.
· How to maximise the positive aspects of your motivational type to massively improve your performance as a coach.

**Don't take our word for it – read what our clients have to say-**

*"An excellent event, I would recommend it to others! I will use these tools in session with my team and informally in my interaction with many people in the organisation and to coach myself."*

**Debbie Bailey Human Resources Director Champneys Health Resort**

*"I now understand what makes people tick! I can bring coaching alive!"*

**Damien Cooper National Business Development Manager Barclays Bank PLC**

**See our website www.rc60s.com for an abundance of testimonials from clients**

**We guarantee that the programme will be:**

1: Practical and relevant training solutions immediately transferable to the workplace
2: New and exciting for all participants regardless of their level of experience
3: Delivered by trainers who have personal experience of business coaching in senior leadership roles
4: Content rich - participants are left in no doubt as to the value and benefits of the training they have received
5: Training that increases performance AND reduces stress at the same time
6: Guaranteed to improve coaching performance

**You get at least 10 times your money's worth!**

Anne offers a maximum of two public seminars each month and limits the number of people in each seminar to guarantee that everyone receives personal attention.

### In summary, here's what you get:

A one-day training programme presented by the founder and author of Results Coaching in 60 Seconds© with information to cover 350 coaching tools and techniques.

A 8-week follow-up email coaching course, Personal Enneagram profiling and One-to-One coaching with our master trainers

PLUS a free coaching toolkit and a 2-hour follow-up teleclass, and a free copy of the 250-page Results Coaching in 60 Seconds e-Book.

**"Your complete satisfaction is important to us."**
**"If you aren't absolutely thrilled with our product by lunchtime of this event, we'll refund 100% of your purchase price. No questions asked."**
**"You don't have to decide now if this product is for you. Just book your place now. If it doesn't do everything I say and more within the first 3 hours, or if you don't absolutely love it, just let me know and we'll give back every penny! So you have nothing to lose and everything to gain."**

**Visit our website now to reserve your place(s) at our next event**
# www.rc60s.com

# RESULTS COACHING
## IN 60 SECONDS

960 Capability Green
Luton
Beds
LU1 3PE
UNITED KINGDOM
Tel: 044 (0) 1582 635032
Fax: 044 (0) 1582 635312

*Remember you are in <u>partnership</u> with the people
in your team that you serve.*